# I Want To Reach
## Your Mind ...

### Where Is It Currently Located?

# I Want to Reach Your Mind ...

## Where Is It Currently Located? ©

### More Incredibly Brilliant Thoughts ®

*By*

# Ashleigh Brilliant

Creator of Pot-Shots® and Author of
*I May Not Be Totally Perfect, but Parts of Me
Are Excellent.*©

**Special Bonus Feature:** *Foreign language translations!*
   To help enrich your travels, studies, and friendships,
every Pot-Shot® in this book comes with its own
translation into Spanish, French, or German.

# Woodbridge® Press

Santa Barbara, California 93102

*Published by*

Woodbridge Press Publishing Company
Post Office Box 209
Santa Barbara, California 93102

*Distributed simultaneously in the United States and Canada.*

Printed in the United States of America.

**Library of Congress Cataloging-in-Publication Data**

Brilliant, Ashleigh, 1933-
    I want to reach your mind—where is it currently located? : more incredibly brilliant thoughts / by Ashleigh Brilliant.
        p.        cm.
    ISBN 0-88007-203-2 : $14.95. — ISBN 0-88007-204-0 (pbk.) : $7.95
    1. Epigrams, American. I. Title.
PN6281 . B6848    1933                              93-36992
818'.5402—dc20                                         CIP

*POT SHOTS and BRILLIANT THOUGHTS*
    *are Registered Trade Marks.*

*Reprint Credits:*
    Page 16: by permission of *The Wall Street Journal.* Copyright © 1992, Dow Jones & Company, Inc. All Rights Reserved Worldwide.
    Page 18: by permission of *People Weekly.* Copyright © 1992, Time-Life, Inc. All Rights Reserved Worldwide. Photo: Jim McHugh/LaMoine.

# Dedication

This book is dedicated to
BARRY CANTOR
who does such a great job
of being my cousin
that, if it were possible,
I'd promote him
to some closer relationship

# Acknowledgements

Special Thanks to

*Amy Stevens,* for celebrating me so spectacularly on the front page of the *Wall Street Journal.*

*Addison Fischer,* for heightening my flights of fancy with a very fancy balloon flight.

*Lawrence Blaustein,* of Lawrence Product Development, Cleveland, Ohio, for grandly conceiving exciting new product possibilities for Brilliant Thoughts®.

*Lee Majors,* for paying so handsomely to quote one Brilliant Thought on TV.

*The Lily Dale Assembly,* for a very spirited reception of my materialization in Lily Dale, New York.

*Caroline and Michael Norris* of Willits, California, for publishing my Thoughts in the attractive form of magnetized messages called "Magnetic Graffiti®."

*Steven Gilbar* (*The Reader's Quotation Book.* Pushcart Press, 1990) and Eric Marcus (*Expect The Worst—You Won't Be Disappointed.* HarperCollins, 1992), for including me with some very distinguished company in their respective collections of quotations. And Don Herron (*The Literary World of San Francisco.* City Lights Books, 1985) for helping to solidify my niche in literary history.

*Rudi Volti,* Professor of Sociology, Pitzer College, Claremont, California, for making his lucky students the first ever required to read me.

*Ruth Dayes,* for sending me the world's most creative mail-orders, (plus chocolate).

My faithful helper *Sue McMillan,* for still being there.

My wife *Dorothy,* for twenty-five years (so far) of the better and the worse.

And, for their respective contributions in translating the epigrams in this book:

Translators: *Spanish:* Carlos Cerecedo; *French:* Francois Bakhouche; *German:* Matthias Rosenthal. (With additional very valuable linguistic assistance from *Martin Needler, Jan Knippers Black, Elizabeth Delatorre, Muriel Garcia, Kerry Carroll, Joëlle Halin, Greti Campbell, Ronald Stern, and Pia Woolverton*).

And also (with just as much reason, and no less appreciation) to:

Lynn Brandenburg, Barney Brantingham, Herb Caen, Allen Carrico, Jim Chastain, Bill Cumiford, Virginia Dean, Carol Fellman, Tod Forman, Don Fraser, "Baron" Ron Herron, the Herb Hobler Family, Steve Hoegerman, Walt Hopmans, Kevin Kellett, Hartley and Jane Kern, Jay and Sandy King, David Krieger, Janet Langley, Burke LeSage, Don Mc-Donald, Ugo Melchiori, Winston Miller, Sol Morrison, Marianne Partridge, Fred Salter, Roger and Nancy Sharp, Jon Thornburgh, Don Voegele, Madeleine Walker, the Howard Weeks Family, Martha U. Wellington, Steve "Flash" Worldie, and Irwin Zucker.

# Contents

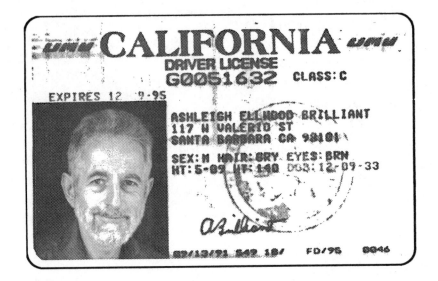

POT-SHOTS NO. 527

I WANT
TO REACH
YOUR MIND —

WHERE
IS IT
CURRENTLY
LOCATED?

Ashleigh
Brilliant

©BRILLIANT ENTERPRISES 1974

Introduction

# Consider Yourself Greeted*

This is ridiculous! Here am I, once again shamelessly shaking out my mind in a public place—and here are you, by your very presence, providing me with aid and encouragement. Why are we doing this? What justification can there possibly be for yet another—(the eighth!)—collection of Brilliant Thoughts®? Don't worry—I have thought of one, and will shortly share it with you.

But first, since this is an Introduction, I must furnish a little orientation for the benefit of newcomers. (Oldcomers, please bear with me.)

To begin with, who is this "I" who is (am) addressing you? In this case, it is an actual person with the honest-to-goodness natal name of Ashleigh Brilliant**—British by birth (1933), American by kind permission of the U.S. Immigration and Naturalization Service (1969), a shining or defective product (depending on your point of view) of numerous educational institutions, and since 1973 a generally harmless resident of Santa Barbara, California.

Next, what exactly are Brilliant Thoughts® (also known as Pot-Shots®), and what makes each of them different from any other kind of thought? To answer this question, you must apply to any suspect item the following tests:

(1) Is it truly original? Does it differ substantially from anything anyone—even yours truly—has ever said before?

(2) Does it contain no more than seventeen words (in the English version)?

(3) Are those words written so as to be easily translatable into other languages?

*Pot-Shot # 162

**For evidence, see Driver's License, opposite.

(4) Are the words capable of being appreciated even without any illustration?

(5) Do they say something really worth saying, and do they say it in the best possible way?

(6) Could you (if you stretched your mind a little) think of it as a kind of one-line poem?

(7) Does it have its own copyright notice, and does my name appear with it?

If it survives intense grilling on all these counts, you can be pretty sure that what you are scrutinizing is the genuine article—or else a fiendishly clever counterfeit.

You should also know that in 1979 the U.S. Library of Congress officially classified Brilliant Thoughts® as Epigrams. That was how I discovered myself to be an Epigrammatist—apparently the world's only full-time professional.* I also now claim to be the world's highest-paid writer (per word), thanks to the Hallmark Card Company, and the world's most quotable author, thanks to *Reader's Digest* magazine.** Through the miracles of licensing, syndication, and self-promotion, you will find my works (if you look hard enough) in and on a wide variety of publications and products. But their original (and, to me, still most comfortable) form is a series of postcards, which keeps every one of the thousands of Brilliant Thoughts® permanently in print. These cards are all available through a unique mail order service, which, as its proprietor, I can of course wholeheartedly recommend. (For details, see Over to You, p. 168.)

Finally, before turning to new developments, I must here, in the interests of good health, and to protect myself from any legal repercussions, offer a word of caution: *The mental morsels contained in this book are heavily impregnated with meaning. Don't try to ingest too many of them at once. The consequences can be very serious.* Our nation's hospital

*It was similarly only from an external authority—the *San Francisco Examiner*—that I had earlier (1967) learned that I was a Hippie. See *Be A Good Neighbor And Leave Me Alone,* p. 93.

**For details, see Book V, p. 10, and Book VII, p. 12.

emergency rooms are busy enough already, without the additional burden of readers who have overdosed on my Epigrams.

## A Gift of Tongues

With those matters disposed of, I can now reveal my exciting new excuse for taking this show once more on the road: As indicated above, it has always been my desire and intention eventually to have all these Thoughts circulating through time and space in all known and unknown languages—and I have carefully crafted them to facilitate this process, completely avoiding rhyme, rhythm, puns, idioms, and all other kinds of word-play which might complicate the task of a translator.

As you might imagine, these self-imposed restrictions have made my own task much harder. Ironically, however, in all the years since Pot-Shots® began to appear in 1967, and despite the best efforts of my publisher to make the necessary arrangements, (resulting in some tantalizingly close calls), no authorized version, in book form, in any other language, has yet appeared. While I was brooding over this painful fact, it occurred to me that there was at least one thing I could do about it: I could insist that any new English-language collection of Brilliant Thoughts® must contain some of *its own translations*. Such a feature would serve various purposes:

(1) It would demonstrate the built-in universality of these expressions and help start the translation ball rolling, perhaps inspiring foreign publishers to start producing their own editions.

(2) It would enable you, the reader, to share these Thoughts with people who don't speak English, and maybe even to use the book, when travelling, as an unconventional kind of phrase-book.

(3) It could be of special value to language students and to their teachers, the best of whom are no doubt always looking for exciting new ways to enliven their lessons.

(4) It would definitely set this volume apart from all its

predecessors, and thereby, at least in my own mind, justify its existence.

Having thus eased my conscience about bringing an eighth brain-child into this cruel world, and having then succeeded in persuading my publisher to take such an adventurous step, I next had to decide which languages would be the lucky ones to embody the first official translations. After much agonizing, I selected three: Spanish, French, and German—the most widely-spoken languages (in addition to English) of the current European Economic Community, whose historic Single Market, perhaps providentially, came into effect in the very year this book was to be published (1993), thereby opening up a vast new area to all kinds of commercial and cultural pioneering.

I myself am, regrettably, not fluent in any of these languages, though I can smatter in French a little more readily than in either of the others. But, by working with various translators, I have made an earnest effort to see that my meaning comes clearly across in all three. For the sake of cultural parity and fair play, you will find that each language has been let loose upon an equal segment of this volume, i.e. a randomly-assigned group of four consecutive chapters.

If you like this special new feature—brought to you at enormous cost—I hope you'll let me know what it has meant to you, and how you've used it. If it means little, nothing, or less than nothing to you, there is, of course, no penalty (other than breaking my heart) for ignoring the whole thing.

## It Themes to Me

Thoughts in general are not orderly things, and those which populate my own upper story ferociously resist all attempts to shepherd and label them. Nevertheless, in order to preserve a semblance of organization, each of my chapters is once again at least loosely linked with some particular topic. And for those readers who would lose sleep unless there were also some overall theme, the momentous linguistic experiment which I have described above irresistibly suggested the leitmotif of: *Communication.*

With that in mind, you may like to know about my appearance in July 1992, as a guest lecturer at a quaint old settlement in western New York State called Lily Dale, which was founded, and is still entirely inhabited, by believers in Spiritualism. As far as I could tell, I performed satisfactorily in this strange setting. But, as one who has always believed in dealing with no more than one world at a time, I found it a little daunting trying to illuminate people who were already sold on something so dazzling as direct communication with departed spirits, and who sometimes even claimed to be practising that art right in front of me.

I never did find out exactly what had moved this devout group to seek out a skeptic like me, but a likely explanation (since this sort of thing has happened before) is that their interest was triggered when somebody came across some one of my thousands of messages which just happened to strike a particularly responsive chord. In this case, I enjoy thinking that it may have been Brilliant Thought #1213: "Communication with the dead is only a little more difficult than communication with some of the living."

## Surprising Rising

My own efforts at reaching out usually confine themselves to a more earthly context, but, within that theater, the sky is the limit. The climb towards my long-declared goal of the Nobel Prize for Literature continues to be very tortuous. Early in 1993, I felt I had attained a milestone of sorts when word came that some of my work had for the first time been selected as required reading in a legitimate college course. But the honor might have been more significant if the required exposure had been to any or all of these volatile volumes of illustrated epigrams. Instead, the work chosen turned out to be my comparatively pedestrian historical study of the Automobile and its Social Effects in California.*

*The Great Car Craze: *How Southern California Collided with the Automobile in the 1920's* (Woodbridge Press, 1989), required in the "Cars and Culture" Course, Department of Sociology, Pitzer College, Claremont, California.

## Growth Formulas

### Democratic Candidates Offer Host of Proposals To Spark the Economy

From Spending to Tax Cuts, Their Ideas Reach a Public That's Eager for Solutions

Fondness for Easier Money

By ALAN MURRAY
Staff Reporter of THE WALL STREET JOURNAL

When it comes to economic policy, the 1992 election campaign...

## What's News—
* * *

### Business and Finance

STOCK PRICES LEAPED again in heavy trading, sending the Dow Jones Industrials up 29.07 points to close at 3201.48, for their sixth consecutive record. The average has surged 297.12 points, or 8.9%, since the Fed cut interest rates on Dec. 26. Other gauges also set records; the Amex index broke a 27-month-old high.

### World-Wide

BUSH OPENED a two-day visit to South Korea that will focus on security matters.

## The Outlook

### Interest-Rate Cuts Still Can Work Magic

WASHINGTON

The Federal Reserve's big gamble is paying off.

By AMY STEVENS
Staff Reporter of THE WALL STREET JOURNAL

SANTA BARBARA, Calif. — Here's a quiz, and a money answer could cost you thousands of dollars.

## Cut Down

### Timber Town Is Bitter Over Efforts to Save The Rare Spotted Owl

As Logging Jobs Disappear, Economy of Forks, Wash., Sinks, and So Do Its Spirits

Contempt for 'Tree Huggers'

By CHARLES McCOY
Staff Reporter of THE WALL STREET JOURNAL

FORKS, Wash. — The dark, damp forests that stretch across the Olympic Peninsula...

### There Are 5,632 Brilliant Thoughts, All Written by Ashleigh Brilliant

### Exactly How Many Brilliant Thoughts Are There? 5,632

Mr. Brilliant Wrote Them— And Copyrighted Them; You Must Know No. 1041

## TODAY'S CONTENTS

Nevertheless, reluctant Academia is being steadily infiltrated by these Thoughts, especially in the pages of textbooks and other scholarly works, whose authors increasingly ply me with requests for permission to illumine their prose with particular Pot-Shots®. (In case you require proof, I have supplied an entire Appendix, almost bursting with details. See Permission Fruition, p. 167.)

Let the record also show that a single Brilliant Thought recently achieved the dramatic distinction of becoming the first ever to be quoted, by permission, in a major television production—and that, for sanctioning this one usage, the author secured a license fee of $5000.* Forgive my fantasies, but, at that rate, the total one-time quotation value of all the Pot-Shots® I have published thus far now exceeds thirty million dollars.

Recognition has also been emanating from some even more surprising sources. On January 6, 1992, I awoke to find myself the subject of a front-page feature article in—of all places—the *Wall Street Journal.* That majestic organ of the business and financial establishment chose to focus upon the copyright protection which has enabled me to win a whole series of legal cases against various infringers of my Epigrams. (See illustration, p. 16.) Two months later, the gossipy weekly magazine, *People,* reaching quite another kind of mass readership, paid me the tribute of full-page treatment.** (See illustration, p. 18.) But I was slightly disappointed when I found that the words "THE SEXIEST MAN ALIVE," emblazoned on the cover of that issue, referred not to me, but to an actor who was the subject of another article.

The glare of all this limelight has so far had little effect upon my very modest lifestyle and demeanor. One remarkable experience did result, however: my first ascent in a hot-air balloon (Dayton, Ohio, July 18, 1992)—the treat of a

*#1336: "We've been through so much together—and most of it was your fault," spoken by "Ski" in "The Journey" episode of the *Raven* detective-adventure series.
**March 16, 1992, p.73

# MODERN WITERATURE

Phrasemaker Ashleigh
Brilliant coins epigrams
that would drive Oscar wild

**W**E'VE BEEN THROUGH SO MUCH TO-
gether, and most of it was your
fault.

Interesting, no?

*Some people should be required to wear warning signs.*

Insightful, yes?

*This started out to be a good day — but then I got up.*

No, the right word is Brilliant — not brilliant as in genius, but Brilliant as in Ashleigh Brilliant, coiner of these and almost 6,000 other salable sayings over the last quarter-century. Brilliant, 58, calls himself the world's only professional epigrammatist, and, working three months out of the year, pulls down $100,000 per annum publishing his minimaxims, which he calls, naturally, Brilliant Thoughts.

"Nobody else seems to be able to do what I do," says Brilliant. "It's much harder than it looks." He adds, sort of epigrammatically, "Brevity is not an indication of superficiality."

The London-born Brilliant began putting his thoughts on postcards in 1967 and selling them in drugstores, student stores and bus stations in the San Francisco Bay Area. That first year, he had only 20 publishable — and copyrighted — thoughts. Now he comes up with more than 300 a year. He has published seven books of his wisdom, and the numbered postcards — which he calls Pot-Shots — sell in thousands of outlets worldwide. He also is syndicated in 14 newspapers. So far, "I may not be totally perfect, but parts of me are excellent," coined in 1973, is probably his most famous line.

Like all artistic trailblazers, Brilliant had to set the rules for his new form. Very early on, he says he decided to limit himself to 17 words per saying, partly because haiku poetry contains 17 syllables. He also avoids puns or slang or any reference to trends — in an effort to keep his work, as he says, "universal."

**A** "My goal is to win the Nobel Prize for Literature," says Ashleigh, brilliantly.

Brilliant often cribs the artwork from so-called clip art — books of uncopyrighted, generic drawings — and then copyrights the whole package. He rationalizes this by saying: "All I feel is admiration for the dead artists and pleasure at being able to rejuvenate their work."

When he's not working, Brilliant and his wife, Dorothy, 60, travel a lot — mainly to exotic locations. But on the job, Brilliant is single-minded.

holing up in a cramped room above the garage of his cottage in Santa Barbara, Calif. Inspiration can come from anywhere — overheard conversations, talk radio, books, movies. "I just sort of get into a rhythm when I'm doing these full-time," he says. "I never have writer's block."

As for the future, well Pot-Shot No. 5,000 may have an answer: *I must stay alive until my work is done — but after that, what excuse will I have?* ∎

3/16/92 PEOPLE

generous *Journal*-reading admirer.* The most thrilling part of the ride in that funny little wicker basket was the descent—coming down onto a quiet street in an ethnically diverse neighborhood, where many of the inhabitants rushed out of their houses and stood around almost reverently to greet the strangers whose unusual craft had so suddenly appeared in their midst. For a moment, I had an inkling of how Columbus must have felt in at least slightly similar circumstances.

## Troubled Waters

Not all the reverberations of my fame have been so upbeat. For example, it recently came to my attention that my name and one of my Pot-Shots are mentioned in a current popular work in the "true crime" genre about a celebrated murder case of the 1980's in Detroit, Michigan.** It seems I owe this distasteful piece of notoriety to the fact that the remains of the unfortunate victim were identified partly by a copy of one particular Pot-Shot, which he was known to have carried in his wallet. (To satisfy your curiosity, it happened to be #1567: "One of my favorite places in the world is wherever you are." This will save you reading the book, which contains nothing else of any possible interest to any nice person.)

As if such stateside exploits were not enough, my quest for the wild Epigram has seen me hunting in some very strange places abroad. One expedition, in 1991, actually took me to Tibet, that fabled land of enlightenment. Upon reaching remote and forbidding Lhasa, however, my muse was soon subdued when I found myself lodged in—of all places—a Holiday Inn—additionally remote in itself (from everything else in the city), and crammed with tourists, all of

---

*It was actually part of a multi-balloon event, with my wife Dorothy flying simultaneously in another balloon, thus inspiring the cover illustration for this volume.

**Masquerade, by Lowell Cauffiel. Hard-cover edition: Doubleday, 1988, p. 285. Paperback: Zebra Books, p. 394.

us being thus frequently reduced to seeking enlightenment from each other.

That same journey did however produce one moment of genuine brightness, if not total illumination, which must be reported here, since it was one of the few times in my life when fate has permitted me to perform the role of a hero:

It occurred in the Himalayan foothills one evening, when my tour-group of eleven tired, hungry, travellers from Santa Barbara, was arriving after dark at a hotel which happened to be situated on a small island in a lake. To our dismay, we found that the ferry, our only access to the hotel, consisted of nothing more trustworthy than a small square wooden raft, on which there was barely room for us all to stand, together with our luggage and the native ferry-man, whose only means of propulsion was simply by pulling on a long rope connected to either shore.

The craft seemed dangerously overloaded, and would surely never have passed any safety inspection in the comfortable Western world which we had so recently left behind. As it carried us out into the darkness, and we all shrank back as far as possible from the unprotected sides, where the water was literally lapping at our feet, I could not only feel the fear in myself, but I could sense it in my companions. This, we were no doubt all thinking, could so easily turn into some horrible headline in our home town newspaper—one which we would never read.

Then it happened. Something suddenly moved me to start singing—and out I came with that rousing old spiritual, "Michael, Row The Boat Ashore," with its beautiful message of faith in "crossing over" safely to another shore in a better world. Others joined in—and immediately, almost miraculously, the tension began to subside. For once, I had the radiant feeling that I had done the right thing at a critical time. We all knew then that we were going to make it across. We could even laugh, after I came to the lines,

*Jordan River deep and wide—*
*Milk and honey on the other side,*

when one of the larger ladies in the group, who had been listening but not singing, exclaimed feelingly, "Milk and Honey!—is *that* all?" Like the rest of us, she was clearly looking forward, (at least that night), to something much more substantial on that other shore.

* * * * *

Strangely enough, it was only a few weeks later that I myself was actually crossing the real Jordan River (on a bridge) on a very different kind of journey. This time I was a member of a group of American "citizen diplomats," who were seeking to do something of a practical nature to help bring peace to one of the most tense and troubled regions of the world. But it was soon only too clear that none of us knew the song which could calm the tensions there.

## The Ill Wind

Even in my own community, my celebrity status (such as it is) has not so far enabled me to have much influence on the crucial issues of our time. For years I have been the leader of a local campaign to control or eliminate the plague of portable dirt-blowing devices (euphemistically called "leaf-blowers") whose noise and dust pollute our otherwise peaceful neighborhoods.* But in this confrontation, the blowers have so far won every round. And the notable example I have long set of preferring to walk or bicycle rather than use any form of motorized transportation for short distances has, as of this writing, had no evident effect upon anyone I know—not even my wife.

## Mind Over Matter

It seems that reaching other people's minds must always be a hit-and-miss affair—one reason why Pot-Shots® seems such an appropriate name for my principal product—and sometimes it's the hits which surprise me most. Take what happened recently, when I accidentally discovered, in a remote corner of a Santa Barbara hillside park, a half-buried

---

*Cf. Pot-Shot #4108: How can noisy machines help clean the world, when noise itself is a form of filth?

Fallen sculpture, later repaired and restored to its lofty perch through some Brilliant efforts (see p. 23).

colossal stone head. As later research established, this object had been carved some 65 years earlier as a memorial to an eminent botanist. It had been set up on a rocky outcrop overlooking the city, then apparently thrown down by vandals, and forgotten so completely that nobody I told about it had ever heard of it.

Surely, I felt, this amazing monument ought to be re-erected—but that seemed an almost impossible task. Physically, it was challenging enough, and would involve lifting a 2½ ton, precariously-situated object up a treacherous slope, to the top of an almost perpendicular boulder. But I knew that by far the hardest part would be first moving all the *minds* necessary to get authorization, assistance, and equipment. Previous experience with the City and its bureaucracy left me very pessimistic, especially if municipal funds were to be involved.

Yet within an astonishingly short time after I announced my discovery to the local media, the "Great Stone Head" was back on its pedestal, cleaned up, fastened down, and even with its broken nose replaced—and all at no cost to the City! How did this come about?—Simply because, by good fortune, I happened to reach exactly the right minds. The great botanist had happened to be an Italian. Santa Barbara happens to have a large Italian community, who, as soon as they learned about the lost head of Francesco Franceschi, determined to restore it. If faith can move mountains, ethnic pride, I discovered, could at least move one large piece of stone.

\* \* \* \* \*

That unaccustomed success has now emboldened me to try to reach one more very important mind, namely yours. Since we've also reached the end of the Introduction, I can only hope that by this point we are at least communicating to some extent. No doubt there is much more that I should know about your mind. But any further progress along those lines will necessarily have to wait until we both discover exactly where it is located.

\* \* \* \* \*

© ASHLEIGH BRILLIANT 1991

I'M
A MUCH
BETTER
PERSON

WHEN I'M NOT
IN MY
RIGHT MIND.

*Ashleigh Brilliant*
SANTA BARBARA

Soy una mejor persona
cuando no estoy bien
de mi cabeza derecha.

# I. Self Expressions

Let's begin our fun-filled foray into the complex world of Communication by making one thing very clear (or at least trying to): If you want to communicate with others, you'd better be sure that you're effectively communicating with yourself. Even if you're not one of those exceptional individuals who have to cope with multiple selves, this can be a very challenging task. Your self may have had a bad day (or a bad life), and be not at all interested in hearing from you. Or at the other extreme, (but equally unreachable), your self may have achieved some totally sublime level of being, but forgotten to leave a forwarding address.

Once you do manage to make contact, there is still the sticky question of what to say to yourself. After all, what information can you give yourself that you don't already know? What jokes can you tell yourself that you haven't probably heard before?

Perhaps it's best, at least on the initial encounter, to let your self do most of the talking. Who knows, something may emerge which will totally surprise you. It was in fact from my own self that I received most of the self-searching insights in this first chapter. But where exactly they came from before that is still something of a mystery to both of us.

© ASHLEIGH BRILLIANT 1991.  POT-SHOTS NO. 5556.

# I AM
# TIRED OF
# BEING ME
# ALL BY
# MYSELF ~

## APPLICATIONS
## FOR ASSISTANCE
## ARE NOW
## BEING ACCEPTED.

*Ashleigh Brilliant*
SANTA BARBARA

Estoy cansado de estar
siempre solo—
se aceptan solicitudes
de ayuda.

© ASHLEIGH BRILLIANT 1976
SANTA BARBARA  POT- SHOTS NO. 976.

# GET ME
# TO A FRIEND!

## MY LONELINESS — PANGS
## ARE COMING
## MORE AND MORE
## FREQUENTLY.

*Ashleigh
Brilliant*

¡Llévenme con un amigo!
Mis calambres de soledad
me vienen
más y más frecuentemente.

POT-SHOTS NO. 1250.

# A TERRIBLE THING
# HAS HAPPENED ~

# I'VE LOST
# MY WILL
# TO SUFFER.

*Ashleigh
Brilliant*
SANTA BARBARA
© BRILLIANT ENTERPRISES 1977.

Una cosa terrible
ha ocurrido—
he perdido mis deseos
de sufrir.

UNKNOWN
TO THE
PUBLIC
AT
LARGE,

FOR YEARS
I HAVE BEEN
QUIETLY
WASTING
MY TIME.

Ashleigh
Brilliant
SANTA BARBARA

©ASHLEIGH BRILLIANT 1977

Sin que el público
en general se enterase,
durante años he estado
perdiendo
mi tiempo calladamente.

HOW
CAN I
CHALLENGE
MYSELF,

Ashleigh
Brilliant

WHEN
I KNOW
I'M ONLY
BLUFFING?

©ASHLEIGH BRILLIANT 1977
SANTA BARBARA

¿Como me voy a desafiar
a mi mismo,
si ya sé que usaré recursos
falsos?

©ASHLEIGH BRILLIANT 1980
SANTA BARBARA

MY RESEARCH
CONSISTS OF
STUDYING
THE EFFECTS
OF PUTTING
SOMEBODY LIKE ME
INTO
A WORLD LIKE THIS.

Ashleigh
Brilliant

Mis estudios consisten en
averiguar los efectos
de poner a alguien como yo
en un mundo como este.

© ASHLEIGH BRILLIANT 1970

POT-SHOTS NO. 146.

I MAY NOT
BE EASY
TO REACH,
BUT I MAY BE
WORTH IT.

Ashleigh Brilliant
SANTA BARBARA

A lo mejor yo no sea
fácil de alcanzar,
pero quizá valgo la pena.

Ashleigh Brilliant

POT-SHOTS NO. 2031

IT'S REMARKABLE
HOW MUCH
HUMANITY
HAS
ACCOMPLISHED,
AND
HOW LITTLE
I HAVE.

© ASHLEIGH BRILLIANT 1980
SANTA BARBARA

Es asombroso todo lo que ha
logrado la humanidad,
y lo poco que yo he logrado.

POT-SHOTS NO. 3970.

I SPEND
ALL MY TIME
TRYING TO
IMPROVE
MYSELF ~

AND THEN
PEOPLE COMPLAIN
THAT I'M
SELF-CENTERED.

© ASHLEIGH BRILLIANT 1985.

Ashleigh Brilliant
SANTA BARBARA

Me paso todo el tiempo
tratando de mejorarme—
y luego la gente se queja
que soy un egocéntrico.

28

**HOW CAN I DO BETTER TOMORROW THAN TODAY,** IF THERE'S NO AGREEMENT ABOUT HOW I DID TODAY?

© ASHLEIGH BRILLIANT 1983.
POT-SHOTS NO. 3164.

Ashleigh Brilliant
SANTA BARBARA

¿Como puedo funcionar
mejor mañana
que hoy, si no hay
acuerdo sobre como
he funcionado hoy?

**I TOO AM ENTITLED TO MY MOMENTS OF SADNESS AND INDECISION.**

© ASHLEIGH BRILLIANT 1983.
POT-SHOTS NO. 2823.

Ashleigh Brilliant
SANTA BARBARA

Yo también tengo derecho
a mis momentos de tristeza
e indecisión.

**IT WOULD SAVE A LOT OF EFFORT,** IF I COULD OPERATE MYSELF BY REMOTE CONTROL.

© ASHLEIGH BRILLIANT 1980.
POT-SHOTS NO. 5041.

Ashleigh Brilliant
SANTA BARBARA

Se ahorraría mucho esfuerzo
si yo pudiera funcionar
por control remoto.

POT-SHOTS NO. 2661.
*Ashleigh Brilliant*

I HAVE
THE REST
OF
MY LIFE
TO IMPROVE ~

BUT
IT MAY
TAKE
LONGER
THAN
THAT.

©ASHLEIGH BRILLIANT 1982.
SANTA BARBARA

Tengo el resto de mi vida
para mejorar— pero quizá
me tome más tiempo que eso.

©ASHLEIGH BRILLIANT 1990.

POT-SHOTS NO 5042.
*Ashleigh Brilliant*
SANTA BARBARA

I BELIEVE IN
SELF-
RELIANCE,

BUT
USUALLY
I NEED
SOMEBODY
TO
HELP ME
RELY ON MYSELF.

Yo creo en la confianza
en mí mismo, pero
generalmente necesito
a alguien que me ayude
a confiar en mí mismo.

*Ashleigh Brilliant*
SANTA
BARBARA

©ASHLEIGH BRILLIANT 1992.

POT-SHOTS NO. 6046.

THIS IS
TERRIBLE!

I'VE
FORGOTTEN
WHY
I HATE
MYSELF.

¡Esto es terrible!
Me olvidé porque me odio.

Quien realmente soy,
es una de esas preguntas
que prefiero dejársela
a los expertos.

¿No lo sabías?—
Hace años que estoy vivo.

Si siempre hiciera lo mejor
de mi, ¿cómo los demás van
a saber que eso es mi mejor?

POT-
SHOTS
NO. 5845

UNFORTUNATELY,
MY ABILITY
TO STAY
UNHAPPY
FOR
LONG PERIODS
OF TIME
HAS
VERY LITTLE
PRACTICAL
VALUE.

©ASHLEIGH BRILLIANT 1992.

Ashleigh Brilliant
SANTA BARBARA

Desafortunadamente,
mi habilidad de sentirme
infelíz durante largos
períodos de tiempo
tiene muy poco valor
práctico.

©ASHLEIGH BRILLIANT 1992. SANTA BARBARA.

POT-SHOTS NO. 5929.

I WANT
TO CREATE
SOMETHING,

BUT CAN'T
FIND ANYTHING
THAT WANTS
TO BE CREATED.

Ashleigh Brilliant

Deseo crear algo,
pero no puedo encontrar
nada que desee
ser creado.

©ASHLEIGH BRILLIANT 1992.

Ashleigh
Brilliant
SANTA
BARBARA

POT-
SHOTS
NO. 5831.

ALL PEOPLE
ARE LIKE ME
IN SOME WAY~
THAT'S WHY I FEEL
SO SORRY FOR EVERYBODY.

Toda gente es como yo
de una manera u otra—
por eso me compadezco
tanto de ellos.

© ASHLEIGH BRILLIANT 1990.  POT-SHOTS NO. 5169.

**AS PART OF A GENERAL AMNESTY, I HAVE DECIDED TO FORGIVE MYSELF.**

Ashleigh Brilliant
SANTA BARBARA

Como parte de una amnistía general, he decidio perdonarme.

POT-SHOTS NO 3022.

Ashleigh Brilliant
SANTA BARBARA

© ASHLEIGH BRILLIANT 1983.

**SOMETIMES I GET VERY TIRED OF ALWAYS BEING ME, AND HAVING THE TIME ALWAYS BEING NOW.**

A veces me canso de ser siempre yo, y que el tiempo sea siempre ahora.

© ASHLEIGH BRILLIANT 1992.  POT-SHOTS NO. 5931.

**Why do I always feel so much better WHENEVER I LOSE MY SELF-CONTROL?**

Ashleigh Brilliant
SANTA BARBARA

¿Porque siempre me siento much mejor después que me descontrolo?

© ASHLEIGH BRILLIANT 1992.    POT-SHOTS NO. 5735.

# I'M NOT MUCH OF A TALKER ~

## BUT I'M NOT MUCH OF A DOER EITHER.

*Ashleigh Brilliant*
SANTA BARBARA

No soy muy hablador—pero tampoco soy muy hacedor.

POT-SHOTS NO. 5743.

# I HAVE LOVED MYSELF AND HATED MYSELF,

## BUT I HAVE NEVER ENVIED MYSELF.

© ASHLEIGH BRILLIANT 1992.

*Ashleigh Brilliant*
SANTA BARBARA

Me he amado y me he odiado, pero jamás me he envidiado.

© ASHLEIGH BRILLIANT 1990.    POT-SHOTS NO. 5094.

# I COULDN'T TEACH ANYBODY ELSE TO BE ME,

## BECAUSE I'M NOT SURE HOW I DO IT MYSELF.

*Ashleigh Brilliant*
SANTA BARBARA

No podría enseñarle a nadie a que sea como yo, porque no estoy seguro como enseñarme a mí mismo.

© ASHLEIGH BRILLIANT 1981

POT-SHOTS NO. 5624.

Ashleigh Brilliant
SANT BARBARA

What shall I do with my God-given lack of talent?

¿Qué haré con mi don natural de falta de talento?

POT-SHOTS NO. 5746. © ASHLEIGH BRILLIANT 1982

There's nothing wrong with being self-centered, if you're centered around a good self.

Ashleigh Brilliant SANTA BARBARA

No tiene nada de malo ser egocéntrico, si ese centro es un buen ego.

© ASHLEIGH BRILLIANT 1983.
SANTA BARBARA

POT-SHOTS NO. 2790.

I AM THE BEST ME IN THE WORLD.

Ashleigh Brilliant

Soy el mejor yo del mundo.

¿Porqué te entiendo
tanto mejor
cuando pierdo todo
contacto
con la realidad?

# II. Two To Tangle

People who have finally succeeded in contacting themselves ought perhaps, in many cases, to stop there. But almost always they then feel the need to communicate with some other individual, thereby creating predicaments of the type which we celebrate (or lament) in the following pages.

Human beings have been saying things to each other for so long that by now one might expect the process to be smooth sailing—but in fact there is no situation more fraught with potential for misunderstanding.

Of course, one of the twists in this tangle is the multiplicity of languages which still bedevils our species, and which can instantly reduce even a highly educated person to the level of a gibbering infant, if he or she doesn't happen to know the local lingo. But even where there is theoretically a common tongue, there is never a common brain. The same words often mean different things to different people, or different things to the same person at different times. Indeed I can think of only two symbolic sounds in the entire human lexicon which seem to have the same meaning to everybody everywhere. One is the telephone dial tone. The other is the sequence of syllables KO-KA-KO-LA.

© ASHLEIGH BRILLIANT 1978.    POT-SHOTS NO. 1448.

*Ashleigh
Brilliant
SANTA BARBARA*

# LET'S RESPECT EACH OTHER'S VIEWS,

## NO MATTER HOW WRONG YOURS MAY BE.

Respetemos
nuestros puntos de vista,
sin importar lo equivocado
que tú estés.

© BRILLIANT ENTERPRISES 1972.    POT-SHOTS NO 399

# YOU'LL NEVER KNOW HOW MUCH I APPRECIATE YOU,

# BECAUSE I'LL PROBABLY NEVER TELL YOU.

*Ashleigh Brilliant
SANTA BARBARA*

Nunca sabrás
cuanto te aprecio,
porque probablemente
nunca te lo diré.

© BRILLIANT ENTERPRISES 1975.    POT-SHOTS NO. 718

*Ashleigh
Brilliant
SANTA BARBARA*

# THANK YOU FOR LEAVING ME ALONE,

## BUT PLEASE DON'T OVERDO IT!

Gracias por
no fastidiarme,
pero por favor no te
excedas.

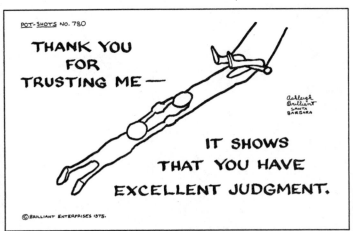

POT-SHOTS NO. 809.

Ashleigh
Brilliant
SANTA BARBARA

# You can always be unfriendly to me —

## that's what friends are for.

Siempre puedes mostrarte
poco amigable conmigo—
para eso somos amigos.

POT-SHOTS NO. 780

# THANK YOU FOR TRUSTING ME —

Ashleigh
Brilliant
SANTA
BARBARA

## IT SHOWS THAT YOU HAVE EXCELLENT JUDGMENT.

Gracias por confiar en mí—
eso demuestra que tienes
un excelente juicio.

POT-SHOTS NO. 946.

# DON'T BE AFRAID TO HURT MY FEELINGS:

Ashleigh
Brilliant

## ALL YOU RISK IS MY UNBOUNDED RAGE.

No temas
lastimar mis sentimientos:
todo lo que arriesgas es
mi ira incontrolable.

Me gustaría
conversar sobre el problema,
tan pronto quites
tus manos de mi garganta.

¿Cómo se siente
ser tú?

BUT HOW DO I KNOW
YOU HONESTLY
WANT ME
TO BE HONEST?

Pero ¿cómo sé
que tú honestamente
deseas que
yo sea honesto?

© ASHLEIGH BRILLIANT 1980.
SANTA BARBARA

POT-SHOTS NO. 1761.

COULD IT
POSSIBLY BE
THAT
YOUR PURPOSE
IN LIFE
IS
TO GIVE ME
TROUBLE?

Ashleigh
Brilliant

¿Es posible que tu propósito en esta vida sea darme problemas?

© ASHLEIGH BRILLIANT 1979

POT-SHOTS NO 1541

Thank you
for giving me
so much
to react against.

Ashleigh
Brilliant
SANTA BARBARA

Gracias por darme tanto para reaccionar en contra.

© ASHLEIGH BRILLIANT 1982.
SANTA BARBARA

POT-SHOTS NO. 2513.
Ashleigh
Brilliant

The
best thing
you can
bring back
from your
trip for me

is you.

Lo mejor que me puedes traer de regreso de tu viaje eres tú.

No es bueno estar de
acuerdo con una persona
que es indecisa.

El hecho que deseo
que estuvieras aquí
no necesariamente significa
que la estoy pasando
de maravillas.

Mis pensamientos tienen
la libertad
de ir a cualquier parte,
pero es sorprendente
lo seguido
que van en tu dirección

POT-SHOTS NO. 5382.

OH HOW I REGRET
THAT I CAN'T
DEVOTE
MY ENTIRE LIFE
TO
YOU AND
YOUR PROBLEMS.

Ashleigh Brilliant
SANTA BARBARA

Ay, como me disgusta
que no puedo dedicar
mi vida entera
a tí y a tus problemas.

POT-SHOTS NO. 2708.

YOU
SEEMED SAD
THAT I
HAD TO
LEAVE,

AND THAT
MADE ME
HAPPY
ALL THE
WAY HOME.

Ashleigh Brilliant

Te ví triste
porque tuve que irme,
y eso hizo feliz
todo el camino a casa.

POT-SHOTS NO. 5400.

DON'T CHANGE
A THING ~

I LIKE
YOUR
INFERIORITY
JUST THE
WAY IT IS.

Ashleigh Brilliant
SANTA BARBARA

No cambies nada—
me gusta tu inferioridad
así como es.

*Two to Tangle  43*

© ASHLEIGH BRILLIANT 1991.  POT-SHOTS NO. 5447.

# WHY DOES OUR BEING TOGETHER

**ALWAYS SEEM TO REQUIRE THE PRESENCE OF A REFEREE?**

*Ashleigh Brilliant*
SANTA BARBARA

¿Porqué cuando estamos juntos siempre parace que requerimos la presencia de un árbitro?

© ASHLEIGH BRILLIANT 1992.  POT-SHOTS NO. 5795.

# IF I CAN'T HAVE YOUR FULL SUPPORT,

**MAY I REQUEST A LITTLE LESS OF YOUR OPPOSITION?**

*Ashleigh Brilliant*
SANTA BARBARA

Si no puedo tener tu apoyo total, ¿puedo pedirte un poco menos de tu oposición?

POT-SHOTS NO. 2843.

# NEVER RESIST A MAD IMPULSE TO DO SOMETHING NICE FOR ME.

© ASHLEIGH BRILLIANT 1983.
SANTA BARBARA

*Ashleigh Brilliant*

Nunca resistas un loco impulso de hacer algo por mí.

44

© ASHLEIGH BRILLIANT 1992.

POT-SHOTS NO 5724.

**I CAN FORGIVE YOU FOR HURTING ME,**

BUT IT'S HARDER TO FORGIVE YOU FOR HURTING YOURSELF.

*Ashleigh Brilliant* SANTA BARBARA.

Te puedo perdonar
por herirme,
pero es más difícil perdonarte
por herirte a tí mismo.

© ASHLEIGH BRILLIANT 1992 SANTA BARBARA

Ashleigh Brilliant

POT-SHOTS NO. 5639.

**I WANT VERY MUCH TO UNDERSTAND YOU,**

BECAUSE FOR ME THAT WOULD BE A TOTALLY NEW EXPERIENCE.

Deseo mucho
entenderte,
porque para mi sería
totalmente
una nueva experiencia.

© ASHLEIGH BRILLIANT 1992.

POT-SHOTS NO. 5721.

**LIKING WHO YOU ARE** IS SOMETIMES MUCH EASIER FOR ME

THAN LIKING WHAT YOU DO.

*Ashleigh Brilliant* SANTA BARBARA

Gustar de quien eres
es alguna veces mas fácil
para mi que gustar
de lo que tú haces.

Tengo el derecho
de arruinar mi vida—
pero tú no tienes el derecho
de ayudarme.

Yo no *te* entiendo,
tú no *me* entiendes—
¿qué más tenemos
en común?

Es tu última oportunidad
de rendirte a mí,
antes que yo me rinda a tí.

Guárdame una buena parte
en tu próximo sueño.

No era realmente yo mismo
hasta que me alejé de tí.

Nunca te olvidaré,
si tu insistes en que te
recuerde.

POT-SHOTS NO. 5090.    © ASHLEIGH BRILLIANT 1990.

# ANYBODY WHO BEHAVED NORMALLY ALL OF THE TIME

## WOULD NOT BE COMPLETELY NORMAL.

*Ashleigh Brilliant*
SANTA BARBARA

Todo aquel que se
comporta normalmente
todo el tiempo no puede
ser totalmente normal.

# III. Psyche Logic

Amid the babble of world tongues, there is one which everybody speaks but nobody really understands: the language of a certain bellicose character, always at war with Reality, known as the Psyche. Intricately encoded in an enigmatic set of directives called Human Nature, it has as yet scarcely begun to be deciphered by scientists (laboring under the tremendous handicap of being Human themselves).

As a species, we are far less well-equipped than most ants to pick up the messages constantly being broadcast by the behavior of our fellows. Many of us have let our antennae deteriorate so sadly that only some such emphatic signal as a kiss or a kick is capable of being perceived, and even then, the exact meaning is liable to be misconstrued.

Under these circumstances, it seems miraculous that any real communication ever takes place at all—yet people do occasionally succeed in sending sparks across those frustrating gaps which inevitably separate one mind from another. Unfortunately, the phenomenon remains rare, partly because many individuals in the world today, to say nothing of tribes and nations, are unwilling to engage in any meaningful dialogue which requires the enormous pre-condition of recognizing each other's existence.

In its incessant struggle to defend its illusions, the Psyche has the capacity to launch whole squadrons of high-flying absurdities—but the complex receiving apparatus of Brilliant Thoughts® is specially tuned to detect and shoot them down. Some of the wreckage is strewn before you in this chapter.

© ASHLEIGH BRILLIANT 1982. POT-SHOTS NO. 5996.

**GOING BERSERK AND RUNNING AMOK**

ARE SIMPLY MY WAY OF COPING WITH THINGS.

*Ashleigh Brilliant*

Volverme loco
y descontrolarme
es simplemente mi manera
de sobrellevar las cosas.

© ASHLEIGH BRILLIANT 1990. POT-SHOTS NO. 5171.

**THE ONLY THING I FEAR IS FEAR ITSELF,**

BUT OF FEAR ITSELF I'M SCARED TO DEATH.

*Ashleigh Brilliant*
SANTA BARBARA

Lo único que temo
es el miedo mismo—
pero el miedo
mismo me atemoriza
a muerte.

© ASHLEIGH BRILLIANT 1990. POT-SHOTS NO. 5175.

**BY THE SHEER FORCE OF MY PERSONALITY,**

I MANAGE TO ALIENATE MOST OF THE PEOPLE I MEET.

*Ashleigh Brilliant*
SANTA BARBARA

Con la simple fuerza
de mi personalidad,
logro alienar a la
mayoría de la gente
que conozco.

Trata de tener una mente abierta—pero no tan abierta que se caiga todo lo que tiene adentro.

No es suficiente tener algo por lo cual luchar—también necesito algo contra que luchar.

Estoy conflictuado por todas las cosas que no deseo hacer.

© ASHLEIGH BRILLIANT 1981.  POT-SHOTS NO. 5413.

You can't have the joy of repenting

unless you sin first.

Ashleigh Brilliant
SANTA BARBARA

No se puede sentir el placer del arrepentimiento, al menos que uno peque primero.

---

© ASHLEIGH BRILLIANT 1991.  POT-SHOTS NO. 5392.

## WHERE DO PEOPLE GO

### TO RECOVER FROM BEING NORMAL?

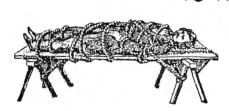

Ashleigh Brilliant
SANTA BARBARA

¿Adónde va la gente para recuperarse de su normalidad?

---

© ASHLEIGH BRILLIANT 1991.  POT-SHOTS NO. 5427.

## I'M ALWAYS LOYAL

### TO WHICHEVER BRAND IS CHEAPEST.

Ashleigh Brilliant
SANTA BARBARA

Soy siempre leal a toda marca que sea la más barata.

© ASHLEIGH BRILLIANT 1992.   POT-SHOTS NO. 5669

## IF I APPEAR DECEPTIVE,

IT'S ONLY BECAUSE I'M NOT YET DECEPTIVE ENOUGH TO CONCEAL IT.

Ashleigh Brilliant
SANTA BARBARA

Si aparento ser ladino,
es porque todavía
no soy lo suficientemente
ladino como para
esconderlo.

© ASHLEIGH BRILLIANT 1967.   POT - SHOTS NO. 29

DON'T LISTEN TO THEIR FOOLISHNESS —

LISTEN TO MINE!

Ashleigh Brilliant
SANTA BARBARA

No escuches
las tonterías de otros—
¡escucha las mías!

© ASHLEIGH BRILLIANT 1992.   POT-SHOTS NO. 6056

Ashleigh Brilliant
SANTA BARBARA

## I'M BLAMELESS~

AND, IN ANY CASE, OTHERS ARE JUST AS MUCH TO BLAME AS I AM.

No es mi culpa—
y si, por si acaso lo fuera,
los demás
tienen tanta culpa como yo.

POT-SHOTS NO 1497

## WHAT I WANT IS TO FEEL BRAVE AND ADVENTUROUS, WITHOUT ACTUALLY HAVING TO RISK ANYTHING.

©ASHLEIGH BRILLIANT 1973. SANTA BARBARA

*Ashleigh Brilliant*

Lo que deseo
es sentirme valiente y
aventurero,
pero sin realmente
tener que arriesgar nada.

POT-SHOTS NO. 1642.

*Ashleigh Brilliant
SANTA BARBARA*

## EACH OF MY FAILURES HAS BEEN AN EXCELLENT PREPARATION FOR THE NEXT ONE.

©ASHLEIGH BRILLIANT 1979.

Cada uno de mis fracasos
ha sido una excelente
preparación
para el próximo.

POT-SHOTS NO. 5877.    ©ASHLEIGH BRILLIANT 1992.

## MY BIGGEST REGRET ABOUT THE THINGS I'VE DONE IS THAT I DIDN'T DO SOME OF THEM SOONER.

*Ashleigh Brilliant
SANTA BARBARA*

Mi gran pesar
sobre las cosas que
he hecho
es que algunas de ellas
no las hice antes.

© ASHLEIGH BRILLIANT 1992.

POT-SHOTS NO. 5791.

WE MUSTN'T ACT HASTILY!

LET'S WAIT UNTIL OUR ENTHUSIASM EVAPORATES.

¡No debemos actuar sin pensar! Esperemos hasta que se evapore nuestro entusiasmo.

© ASHLEIGH BRILLIANT 1981. SANTA BARBARA

POT-SHOTS NO. 2055.

I BELIEVE, WITH GREAT SINCERITY, IN WHATEVER IT WILL BENEFIT ME TO SAY I BELIEVE IN.

Creo, con grand sinceridad, en todo aquello que me beneficie al decir que creo en ello.

© ASHLEIGH BRILLIANT 1980 SANTA BARBARA

POT-SHOTS NO. 1766.

FACTS SHOULD NEVER BE FACED TOO EARLY IN THE MORNING.

Ninguna realidad debe enfrentarse demasiado temprano por la mañana.

© ASHLEIGH BRILLIANT 1981.   POT-SHOTS NO. 2329.

# I CAN ACCEPT THE INCONVENIENT AND THE UNJUST,

BUT I REFUSE TO ACCEPT THE INEVITABLE.

Ashleigh Brilliant
SANTA BARBARA

Puedo aceptar lo inconveniente y lo injusto, pero me rehuso a aceptar lo inevitable.

© ASHLEIGH BRILLIANT 1992.   POT-SHOTS NO. 5637.

# THE REASON I NEVER DO ANYTHING

IS THAT THERE'S ALWAYS SOMETHING ELSE I HAVE TO DO FIRST.

Ashleigh Brilliant
SANTA BARBARA

La razón por la cual nunca hago nada es por que siempre tengo algo que hacer antes.

© ASHLEIGH BRILLIANT 1981.
SANTA BARBARA   POT-SHOTS NO. 2339.

# LET ME KNOW IF THERE'S ANY WAY I CAN RELIEVE YOUR PAIN,

WITHOUT INCREASING MY OWN.

Ashleigh Brilliant

Házme saber si hay alguna manera de aliviar tu dolor, sin aumentar el mío.

POT-SHOTS NO. 2388.

WITH
A LITTLE
MORE
COURAGE,

I COULD
GET MYSELF
INTO
A LOT
MORE
TROUBLE.

© ASHLEIGH BRILLIANT 1982.

Con un poco más de valentía,
me podría meter
en muchos más problemas.

© ASHLEIGH BRILLIANT 1982.
SANTA BARBARA

POT-SHOTS NO. 2417.

WHAT YOU SAY
CAN MEAN
ANYTHING ~

BUT
WHAT
YOU DO

MEANS
EVERYTHING.

Lo que dices
puede significar algo—
pero lo que haces
significa todo.

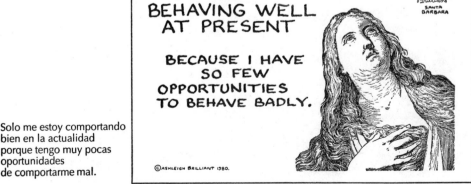

POT-SHOTS NO. 1779.

Ashleigh
Brilliant
SANTA
BARBARA

I'M ONLY
BEHAVING WELL
AT PRESENT

BECAUSE I HAVE
SO FEW
OPPORTUNITIES
TO BEHAVE BADLY.

© ASHLEIGH BRILLIANT 1980.

Solo me estoy comportando
bien en la actualidad
porque tengo muy pocas
oportunidades
de comportarme mal.

© ASHLEIGH BRILLIANT 1982

POT-SHOTS NO. 2583

Ashleigh Brilliant
SANTA BARBARA

## MY EAR IS ALWAYS OPEN FOR APPRECIATION,

## BUT FOR CRITICISM, YOU HAVE TO MAKE AN APPOINTMENT.

Mis oídos siempre están
abiertos para
el reconocimeinto,
pero para la crítica
hay que hacer cita.

© ASHLEIGH BRILLIANT 1987.
SANTA BARBARA

POT-SHOTS NO. 4257.

## THE FUNNIEST THING ABOUT SOME PEOPLE

## IS THAT THEY HAVE NO SENSE OF HUMOR.

Ashleigh Brilliant

Lo más gracioso
de algunas personas
es que no tienen
sentido del humor.

© ASHLEIGH BRILLIANT 1983
SANTA BARBARA

POT-SHOTS NO 2845.

## THE BEST KIND OF SELFISHNESS

is the kind
that gets
selfish
pleasure
from helping
other people.

Ashleigh Brilliant

El mejor egoismo
es el tipo
de placer egoista
de ayudar a los demás.

© ASHLEIGH BRILLIANT 1990.
SANTA BARBARA

POT-SHOTS NO. 5155.

**THERE CAN BE NO MEANINGFUL NEGOTIATIONS,**

UNTIL YOU REMOVE THE PRESSURE WHICH IS FORCING ME TO NEGOTIATE.

*Ashleigh Brilliant*

No pueden haber negociaciones relevantes, hasta que me quites la presión que me está forzando a negociar.

---

© ASHLEIGH BRILLIANT 1990.

POT-SHOTS NO. 5075.

**I MAY NOT HAVE MUCH ELSE TO BE PROUD OF,**

BUT AT LEAST I HAVE MY GRIEVANCES.

*Ashleigh Brilliant*
SANTA BARBARA

Quizá no tengo muchas cosas de que estar orgulloso, pero al menos tengo mis quejas.

---

© ASHLEIGH BRILLIANT 1991.

POT-SHOTS NO. 5564.

**WHEN YOU KNOW EVERYTHING WORTH KNOWING,**

COME TO ME, AND I'LL TELL YOU THE REST.

*Ashleigh Brilliant*
SANTA BARBARA

Cuando sepas todo lo que valga la pena saber, ven a mí, y te contaré el resto.

# Pot-Shots BY ASHLEIGH BRILLIANT

© ASHLEIGH BRILLIANT 1991.

POT-SHOTS NO. 5622.

Ashleigh Brilliant
SANTA BARBARA

## DISTANCES CAN BE DECEPTIVE ~

SOMETIMES
WHEN
I'M CLOSE
TO YOU,

I FIND
YOU'RE
VERY FAR
FROM ME.

Las distancias pueden engañar: algunas veces, cuando más cerca estoy de tí me doy cuenta que estás muy lejos de mí.

# IV. Heart Murmurs

Love is famous for conquering obstacles, yet, when we seek to communicate with our nearest and dearest, it is love itself which only too often gets in the way. Those with whom we are involved most deeply turn out to be those whom it is also hardest to fathom, or be fathomed by. No two hearts speak exactly the same language, and the murmurs of one, even when they manage to be heard by some other heart, inevitably lose something in translation.

But the picture is not totally bleak. With courage and determination, it is sometimes possible to pierce the love barrier and achieve at least some rudimentary degree of mutual comprehension. This can be a dangerous undertaking, because the fabric of love is at certain points extremely fragile. But those who have taken the risk, and succeeded in penetrating a partner's mind to deposit a significant thought, describe the experience in ecstatic terms.

For the rest of us, however (constituting, alas, the vast majority of humankind) communication with the beloved, as documented in this chapter, is for the most part considerably less than rapturous. Only too often, indeed, it must be limited to banalities and trivia, or else (as a last resort) conducted through the good offices of some supposedly neutral third party, such as the family cat.

Ahora, que estamos
enamorados,
¿qué es lo siguiente
que ocurre?

Por favor
atráeme.

Tu amor sería
un buen lugar para
perderme y nunca
encontrar la salida

POT-SHOTS NO. 1471.

YOU WERE MEANT FOR ME

PERHAPS AS A PUNISHMENT.

©ASHLEIGH BRILLIANT 1979 SANTA BARBARA

Tu fuiste hecha para mí,
—quizá como un castigo.

©ASHLEIGH BRILLIANT 1971.

POT-SHOTS NO. 271

YOUR APPLICATION FOR LOVE AND UNDERSTANDING IS CURRENTLY BEING PROCESSED.

Ashleigh Brilliant
SANTA BARBARA

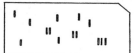

Tu solicitud
por amor y comprensión
está siendo procesada en
estos momentos.

IN ORDER TO RETAIN THE TITLE,

A LOVER MUST KEEP LOVING.

POT-SHOTS NO 1540.

Ashleigh Brilliant
SANTA BARBARA

©ASHLEIGH BRILLIANT 1979.

Para mantener ese
nombre, un amante
debe seguir amando.

POT-SHOTS No. 1600

HOW CAN I GIVE YOU MORE LOVE WITHOUT HAVING TO GIVE YOU MORE TIME?

Ashleigh Brilliant
SANTA BARBARA

© ASHLEIGH BRILLIANT 1979.

¿Cómo puedo darte
más amor,
sin tener que dedicarte
más tiempo?

POT-SHOTS NO. 1890.

Ashleigh Brilliant
SANTA BARBARA

IF NEED MEANS LOVE, I LOVE YOU.

IF LOVE MEANS NEED, I NEED YOU.

© ASHLEIGH BRILLIANT 1980.

Si la necesidad significa
amor, te amo.
Si el amor significa
necesidad, te necesito.

Ashleigh Brilliant
SANTA BARBARA

POT-SHOTS NO. 2046.

THE FACT THAT I'M NOT EXACTLY WHAT YOU'RE LOOKING FOR

MAY BE MORE YOUR FAULT THAN MINE.

© ASHLEIGH BRILLIANT 1980.

El hecho que no soy
exactamente lo que
buscas quizá es más
tu culpa que la mía.

Solo me amas
porque temes no amarme.

Me tomaría mucho tiempo
explicar mis exactos
sentimientos por ti—
digámos que es amor.

De alguna manera, toda
la magia
ha desaparecido de
nuestra separación.

© ASHLEIGH BRILLIANT 1987.  POT-SHOTS NO. 4237.

**SHARING SOMETHING WITH YOU** IS SOMETIMES THE ONLY THING THAT GIVES IT ANY IMPORTANCE.

El compartir algo contigo es a veces lo único que le dá alguna importancia.

POT-SHOTS NO. 5131.  © ASHLEIGH BRILLIANT 1990.

**YOU HAVE THE POWER TO MAKE ME HAPPY ~** BUT IT'S TOTALLY WORTHLESS, UNLESS YOU USE IT.

Tienes el poder de hacerme felíz— pero no sirve de nada al menos que lo uses.

© ASHLEIGH BRILLIANT 1990  POT-SHOTS NO. 5016.

**YOU CAN ALWAYS COME BACK TO ME,** but I can't promise that no questions will be asked.

Siempre puedes volver a mí, pero no te puedo prometer que no se harán preguntas

© ASHLEIGH BRILLIANT 1990.  POT-SHOTS NO. 5107.

Have you ever considered what a rare privilege it is to be personally rejected by me?

Ashleigh Brilliant
SANTA BARBARA

¿Alguna vez has considerado qué raro privilegio es ser personalmente rechazado por mí?

© ASHLEIGH BRILLIANT 1991.  POT-SHOTS NO. 5397.

TO ME, YOU ARE HEAVEN, BUT YOU ARE NOT EXACTLY WHAT I THOUGHT HEAVEN WOULD BE.

Ashleigh Brilliant
SANTA BARBARA

Para mí, tú eres el paraíso, pero no eres exactamente lo que you creía que era el paraíso.

© ASHLEIGH BRILLIANT 1991.  POT-SHOTS NO. 5549.

Ashleigh Brilliant
SANTA BARBARA

THE SECRET OF BEING A GOOD LOVER IS NOT KNOWING WHEN TO STOP.

El secreto de ser un buen amante es el no saber cuando parar.

©ASHLEIGH BRILLIANT 1992.    POT-SHOTS NO. 5754.

Nobody
ever
told me
Love
would be
such
hard work.

*Ashleigh Brilliant*
SANTA BARBARA

Nadie me había dicho
que el amor era
un trabajo tan duro.

©ASHLEIGH BRILLIANT 1992.    POT-SHOTS NO. 5808.

SOMEBODY
HAS STOLEN MY HEART ~

AND YOU
ARE HIGH
ON MY
LIST OF
SUSPECTS.

*Ashleigh Brilliant*
SANTA BARBARA

Alguien
me ha robado el corazón—
y tú estás muy alto
en mi lista de sospechosos.

©ASHLEIGH BRILLIANT 1992.    POT-SHOTS
NO. 5679.

EITHER
I'M YOURS
OR
YOU'RE MINE,

— OR
CAN WE
HAVE IT
BOTH WAYS?

*Ashleigh Brilliant*
SANTA BARBARA.

O soy tuyo o eres mía—
¿o puede ser de la
dos maneras?

© ASHLEIGH BRILLIANT 1992.

POT-SHOTS NO. 5767.

Love never dies a natural death.

Ashleigh Brilliant SANTA BARBARA

El amor jamás muere de causas naturales.

© ASHLEIGH BRILLIANT 1992.

POT-SHOTS NO. 6065.

THE ONLY WAY TO MAINTAIN OUR HONEST RELATIONSHIP

Ashleigh Brilliant SANTA BARBARA

IS BY CONCEALING CERTAIN THINGS FROM EACH OTHER.

La única manera de mantener nuestra relación honesta es escondiendo ciertas cosas el uno del otro.

© ASHLEIGH BRILLIANT 1991

POT-SHOTS NO. 5591.

BEING NUMBER ONE WITH YOU IS NOT ENOUGH ~

I WANT TO BE ALL THE OTHER NUMBERS TOO.

Ashleigh Brilliant SANTA BARBARA

Ser número uno contigo no es suficiente— deseo ser todos los otros números también.

©ASHLEIGH BRILLIANT 1992.          POT-SHOTS NO. 6059.

# I NEED
# MORE
# PRACTICE

## IN
## BEING
## LOVED.

Ashleigh Brilliant
SANTA BARBARA

Necesito más práctica
en ser amado.

©ASHLEIGH BRILLIANT 1992.  SANTA BARBARA          POT-SHOTS NO. 5904.

# YOU'LL
# NEVER
# LOVE ME
# ENOUGH ~

## BUT
## AT LEAST
## MAKE
## A START!

Ashleigh Brilliant

Nunca me amarás lo
suficiente—
¡pero al menos
comienza a amarme!

©ASHLEIGH BRILLIANT 1992. SANTA BARBARA          POT-SHOTS NO. 5887.

# Ever since you abandoned it,
## the
## city
## of
## my heart
## has
## been
## a
## ghost-town.

Ashleigh Brilliant

Desde que
la abandonaste,
la ciudad en mi corazón
es un pueblo fantasma

## NONE OF MY LIFE MAKES ANY SENSE

### EXCEPT THE PART WHERE YOU SAY YOU LOVE ME.

Nada en mi vida
tiene sentido
excepto la parte
donde dices que me amas.

## YOU'RE EVERYTHING I WANT,

### AND, IN ADDITION, YOU'RE SEVERAL THINGS I DON'T WANT AT ALL.

Tú eres todo lo que deseo,
y, además,
eres varias cosas
que no deseo para nada.

## THE SECRET OF OUR WONDERFUL RELATIONSHIP

### IS THAT, MUCH OF THE TIME, IT'S NOT REALLY SO WONDERFUL.

El secreto de
nuestra maravillosa
relación es que,
la mayoría del tiempo,
realmente no es tan
marvillosa.

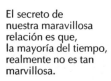

Je n'ai peut-être pas
encore tout,
mais j'ai déjà
trop.

# V. Household Words

We take you now to the home of the modern family—a stronghold on the front line of the great world struggle to communicate. Its hard-wired walls often surround a dazzling stockpile of sophisticated electronic gear, enabling its occupants to send and receive, keep and copy, jiggle and juggle, monstrous amounts of information.

But progress is never uniform, and in many less advanced households such anachronistic transmitting instruments as pens and pencils maintain a lingering presence, while incoming messages still arrive in the antiquated forms of letters and newspapers, still hand-delivered by what at least still appear to be ordinary human beings. Nor has any effective replacement yet been found for that very primitive short-range communication system which uses simple air-vibrations, projected from the sender's unaided larynx, and registering upon the receiver's naked ear.

Never before, however, has it been possible for the average family to take in and give out so much data—and never has there been so little time to do anything with it. Our spouses, our children—probably even our pets --know far more now than spouses, children, or pets have ever been allowed to know in the past. And what is the result?—A society so exhausted by over-communication that at least an occasional day of no news really would be good news.

Failing that, we might at least try limiting all messages to a maximum of seventeen words, as in the following biting bulletins from the home front.

© ASHLEIGH BRILLIANT 1981. SANTA BARBARA          POT-SHOTS NO. 2222.

# I'M GLAD THERE ARE AT LEAST SOME THINGS SOMEWHERE

## THAT I DON'T HAVE TO DO TODAY.

Ashleigh Brilliant

Je suis content qu'il y ait
au moins quelque chose
quelque part que je n'ai pas
à faire aujourd'hui.

© BRILLIANT ENTERPRISES 1975.          POT-SHOTS NO. 810.

# I'VE BEEN MARRIED SO LONG, I'VE FORGOTTEN WHO I AM.

Ashleigh Brilliant
SANTA BARBARA

Je suis marié
depuis si longtemps
que j'ai oublié qui je suis.

© ASHLEIGH BRILLIANT 1980.          POT-SHOTS NO. 1927.

# DONATIONS ARE DESPERATELY NEEDED

## TO SUPPORT MY RECKLESS EXTRAVAGANCE.

Ashleigh Brilliant
SANTA BARBARA

Des donations
sont désespérément demandées
pour supporter
mes folles dépenses.

POT-SHOTS NO. 2284.

Ashleigh Brilliant
SANTA
BARBARA

SOME OF MY PROBLEMS ARE JUST VISITING, BUT SOME HAVE APPARENTLY DECIDED TO MOVE IN WITH ME.

© ASHLEIGH BRILLIANT 1981.

Certains de mes problèmes
me rendent seulement visite,
mais d'autres ont apparemment
décidé d'emménager avec moi.

POT-SHOTS NO. 2718.

Ashleigh Brilliant
SANTA
BARBARA

A CERTAIN GROUP OF GENIUSES CAN EASILY LEARN EVEN THE WORLD'S MOST DIFFICULT LANGUAGES:

THEY'RE CALLED BABIES.

© ASHLEIGH BRILLIANT 1983

Un certain groupe de génies
peuvent facilement apprendre
même les langues les plus
difficiles du monde:
Ils s'appellent des bébés.

© ASHLEIGH BRILLIANT 1983

POT-SHOTS NO. 2722.

Ashleigh Brilliant
SANTA
BARBARA

I don't stop loving people after they die ~ In fact, sometimes they're easier then to love.

Je ne cesse pas d'aimer les gens
—après leur mort—
en fait, ils sont
parfois plus faciles à aimer.

Pourquoi les enfants
ne se battent-ils jamais
pour la garde de leurs parents?

Ne t'inqiète pas—
je resterai avec toi
jusqu'au bout
de ton argent.

Un des moyens de recevoir
plus d'amour des gens est de
faciliter leur amour pour vous.

Le moins de mensonges vous dites, le plus de chances il y a d'être cru
lorsque vous en dites un.

Si seulement ceux qui me sont les plus chers pouvaient être aussi ceux qui sont les plus près.

Les gens qui ne peuvent pas régler leurs problèmes avec succès ne devraient pas avoir le droit d'en avoir.

Chaque famille devrait avoir
un historien,
pour être sûre que son dossier
soit proprement falsifié.

Aucun moment passé
avec un chat sur ses genoux
ne peut jamais être vraiment
considéré comme totalement
gâché.

Accomplissez votre devoir
de citoyen: mariez-vous tôt
et souvent.

# THERE ARE SOME THINGS CHILDREN CANNOT KNOW,

## BECAUSE, ONCE THEY LEARN THEM, THEY ARE NO LONGER CHILDREN.

Il y a des choses
que les enfants ne peuvent pas
savoir,car une fois qu'ils les
apprennent,ce ne sont
plus des enfants.

I HAVE THE KIND OF SISTER

THAT ONLY A SISTER

COULD UNDERSTAND.

J'ai le genre de soeur
que seule une soeur
pourrait comprendre.

# SOME OF THE WORST THINGS EVER DONE TO ME

## WERE DONE WITH THE BEST OF INTENTIONS.

Certaines des pires choses
qui m'aient été faites
l'ont été avec
la meilleure intention.

© ASHLEIGH BRILLIANT 1992.    POT-SHOTS NO. 5656.

# BROKEN HEARTS HEAL SLOWLY,

BUT A SPEEDY APPLICATION OF CHOCOLATE CAN OFTEN HELP STOP THE INITIAL BLEEDING.

Les coeurs brisés se guérissent lentement, mais une application rapide de chocolat peut bien souvent aider à arrêter le saignement initial.

© ASHLEIGH BRILLIANT 1992.    POT-SHOTS NO. 5781.

# SOME OF MY INSTINCTS

TELL ME NOT TO FOLLOW SOME OF MY OTHER INSTINCTS.

Certains de mes instincts me disent de ne pas suivre certains de mes autres instincts.

© ASHLEIGH BRILLIANT 1992.    POT-SHOTS NO. 5842.

# DO UNTO YOUR CHILDREN

AS YOU WOULD WANT THEM TO DO UNTO THEIR CHILDREN.

Agissez envers vos enfants comme vous voudriez qu'ils agissent envers les leurs

© ASHLEIGH BRILLIANT 1992.  POT-SHOTS NO. 6045.

I FIND
BEING
AWAKE
VERY
TIRING.

Ashleigh Brilliant
SANTA BARBARA

Je trouve très fatigant
d'être éveillé.

---

© ASHLEIGH BRILLIANT 1992.  POT-SHOTS NO. 6072.

You can't
always
be right
and be
married.

Ashleigh Brilliant
SANTA BARBARA

Vous ne pouvez pas toujours
avoir raison
et être marié.

---

© ASHLEIGH BRILLIANT 1992.  POT-SHOTS NO. 5765.

Ashleigh
Brilliant
SANTA BARBARA

BY THE TIME
THE YOUNG DISCOVER
THAT
OLD PEOPLE
ARE NOT
REALLY WISER,

THEY ARE
OLD
THEMSELVES.

Quand les jeunes
découvrent enfin que les vieux
ne sont pas plus sages qu'eux,
ils sont eux-mêmes vieux.

POT-SHOTS NO. 2489.

# MY MIND AND HEART SOMETIMES GIVE CONFUSING MESSAGES,

BUT
THE CALL
OF MY STOMACH
IS ALWAYS
CLEAR.

Ashleigh
Brilliant

Mon esprit et mon coeur m'envoient parfois des messages confus, mais l'appel de mon estomac est toujours clair.

# VI. Body Language

If you aren't doing anything else with your body at the moment, permit me to make it the topic of this chapter:

Internally, your communications are quite good, at least to the extent that your left hand usually knows what your right hand is doing. (Whether or not it approves is of course another matter.) There are however certain familiar situations which produce heavy static on the lines—as between your eyes, mouth, and stomach, when the question is what you really should be eating,—or between your heart and your head, when romance is in the offing (or in the on-and-offing.)

The external language of the body, in contrast, often comes through loud and clear, although translation may still be a problem. Facial expressions are, within limits, easily readable, and a knowledge of these is particularly useful to the traveller in foreign lands. The baring of the teeth, for example, can be readily interpreted to mean one of two things: it is either a warm smile of friendship, or a fierce expression of hostility. Even more helpful are such subtle hints as the way people sit, stand, and gesture. Certain gestures, such as punching somebody in the face, can be a dead giveaway of a person's feelings.

But experienced travellers will attest that, of all known body language, the most universally recognized signal is something even more eloquent. It consists of inserting either hand into some cavity in the garments, then withdrawing it and holding it forward, at about eye level, with some money in it.

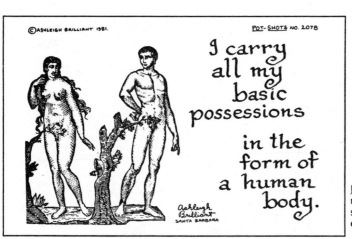

Je transporte tous
mes biens essentiels
sous forme de
corps humain.

Une chose est certaine
au sujet de la mort:
C'est une invalidité
extrêmement inconvéniente.

La chose
la plus efficace
pour préserver ma santé
est ma peur des médecins.

POT-SHOTS NO. 1231.

# I'M ON A SPECIAL MENTAL HEALTH DIET:

## I CAN ONLY EAT WHAT I ENJOY.

Ashleigh
Brilliant

© BRILLIANT ENTERPRISES 1977. SANTA BARBARA

Je suis un régime spécial
pour la santé mentale:
Je ne peux manger que ce qui
me fait plaisir.

---

© ASHLEIGH BRILLIANT 1973
SANTA BARBARA

POT-SHOTS NO. 544

# I COULD LIVE WITHOUT MOSQUITOES,

Ashleigh
Brilliant

## AND ONLY WISH THAT THEY COULD LIVE WITHOUT ME.

Je pourrais vivre sans
moustiques, et je veux
seulement qu'ils
puissent vivre sans moi.

---

© ASHLEIGH BRILLIANT 1980.

POT-SHOTS NO. 1902.

# ONE OF MY CLEVER WAYS OF FIGHTING BACK AGAINST THE WORLD

## IS BY BOLDLY GOING TO BED.

Ashleigh Brilliant
SANTA BARBARA

Une de mes façons
ingénieuses de lutter
contre le monde
est d'aller courageusement
au lit.

©ASHLEIGH BRILLIANT 1985

POT-SHOTS NO. 3934.

# HERE'S WISHING YOU GOOD LUCK

## ON THE OPERATING TABLE

Ashleigh Brilliant
SANTA BARBARA

Je vous souhaite
bonne chance
sur la table d'opération.

---

©ASHLEIGH BRILLIANT 1990
SANTA BARBARA

Ashleigh Brilliant

POT-SHOTS NO. 5283.

# MY LIVING-LICENSE IS PERFECTLY VALID,

## BUT THE EXPIRATION DATE IS ILLEGIBLE.

Mon permis de vivre
est parfaitement en règle,
mais la date d'expiration
est illisible.

---

©ASHLEIGH BRILLIANT 1990.

POT-SHOTS NO. 5083.

# WHAT SHALL I DO? ~

## EVEN MY TOES ARE GETTING OLDER!

Ashleigh Brilliant
SANTA BARBARA

Que faire?
Même mes orteils
deviennent plus vieux!

© ASHLEIGH BRILLIANT 1990.   POT-SHOTS NO. 5312.

I TRY TO AVOID
STRESSFUL
ACTIVITIES ~

Ashleigh
Brilliant
SANTA BARBARA

THAT'S WHY
I HAVE
SO MUCH
FREE TIME.

J'essaie d'éviter
les activités stressantes—
c'est la raison pour laquelle
j'ai tant de temps libre.

POT-SHOTS NO. 5157.   © ASHLEIGH BRILLIANT 1990.

It's very hard
to choose
a specialist
to treat
an ache
in my
soul.

Ashleigh Brilliant
SANTA BARBARA

Il est très dur
de choisir un spécialiste
pour traiter une douleur
de mon âme.

© ASHLEIGH BRILLIANT 1991.   POT-SHOTS NO. 5379.

Ashleigh
Brilliant
SANTA
BARBARA

HEALING
IS
NATURE'S
WAY
OF
TELLING YOU
THAT YOU
REALLY DO
MATTER.

Guérir
est le moyen par lequel
la nature vous signifie que
vous êtes très important.

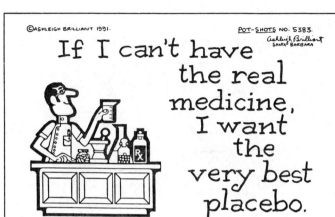

Si je ne peux pas avoir
le vrai médicament,
je veux
le meilleur placebo.

La vie n'est-elle pas
déja assez difficile,
sans faire d'exercice?

En restant en vie trop
longtemps, vous pourriez
sérieusement nuire
à votre santé.

© ASHLEIGH BRILLIANT 1991

POT-SHOTS NO. 5495.

## WE CAN'T YET CURE ALL DISEASES ~

### BUT WE'RE ALREADY EXPERT AT CAUSING MANY OF THEM.

Nous ne pouvons pas encore guérir toutes les maladies—
mais nous sommes déjà experts à en causer beaucoup.

---

POT-SHOTS NO. 5575.

## THERE IS A VAST REGION OF ENORMOUS POTENTIAL

### LOCATED SOMEWHERE BETWEEN YOUR EARS.

© ASHLEIGH BRILLIANT 1991

Il y a une vaste région avec un potentiel énorme située quelque part entre vos oreilles.

---

© ASHLEIGH BRILLIANT 1991.   Ashleigh Brilliant SANTA BARBARA   POT-SHOTS NO. 5506.

## SLEEPING IS A PART OF LIVING ~

### AND, IF DONE WELL, CAN BE ONE OF THE BEST PARTS.

Dormir
fait partie de la vie—
et, si proprement fait,
peut en être
une des meilleures parties.

© ASHLEIGH BRILLIANT 1991.

POT-SHOTS NO. 5521.

# I KNOW I'M IN TROUBLE WHEN MY OWN BODY STARTS TO REJECT ME.

Ashleigh Brilliant
SANTA BARBARA

Je sais que j'ai des ennuis quand mon propre corps commence à me rejeter.

© ASHLEIGH BRILLIANT 1992.

POT-SHOTS NO. 5759.

# NO MATTER HOW RICH YOU ARE,

## YOU CAN'T HIRE ANYBODY TO EXERCISE FOR YOU.

Ashleigh Brilliant
SANTA BARBARA

Aussi riche que vous soyez, vous ne pouvez pas engager quelqu'un pour faire de l'exercice à votre place.

© ASHLEIGH BRILLIANT 1992.

POT-SHOTS NO. 5635.

# THE MOST PRECIOUS DOCUMENT IN THE WORLD

## IS A CLEAN BILL OF HEALTH.

Ashleigh Brilliant
SANTA BARBARA

Le document le plus précieux du monde est un certificat de pleine forme

© ASHLEIGH BRILLIANT 1991.  POT-SHOTS NO. 5603.

**NOTHING COMES OUT OF MY BODY THAT DIDN'T GO IN~**

**BUT EVERYTHING'S SO CHANGED!**

Ashleigh Brilliant
SANTA BARBARA

Rien ne sort de mon corps qui n'y soit pas entré— mais tout a tellement changé!

© ASHLEIGH BRILLIANT 1992.  POT-SHOTS NO. 5726.

**ANYTHING AS POPULAR AS SEX**

**MUST SURELY BE A FAD THAT WON'T LAST.**

Ashleigh Brilliant SANTA BARBARA

Quelque chose aussi populaire que le sexe doit sûrement être une lubie qui ne durera pas.

© ASHLEIGH BRILLIANT 1992.  POT-SHOTS NO. 5689

**THE ONLY REAL CURE FOR SNORING**

**IS DEAFNESS**

Ashleigh Brilliant
SANTA BARBARA

Le seul remède efficace au ronflement est la surdité.

Avoir une bonne nuit
de sommeil
est ce dont j'ai toujours
rêvé.

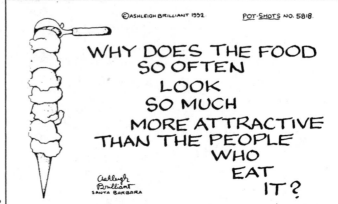

Pourquoi la nourriture
parait-elle si souvent
beaucoup plus attirante
que les gens qui la mangent?

Si la mort
ne résoud pas mes problèmes,
alors je saurai
que j'ai vraiment des ennuis.

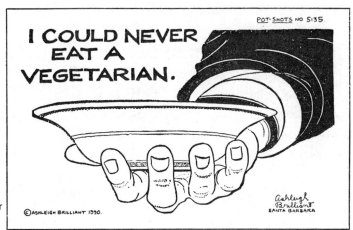

Je ne pourrai jamais manger un végétarien.

Essayez de considérer la mort comme une expérience instructive.

Parfois la meilleure chose que vous puissiez faire pour votre corps est de le laisser tranquille.

POT-SHOTS NO. 5438.

# HOW CAN ANYONE BE HAPPY,

## KNOWING THAT EVERYONE IS NOT HAPPY?

*Ashleigh Brilliant*
SANTA BARBARA

Comment quiconque
peut-il être heureux,
sachant que tout le monde
ne l'est pas?

# VII. Upon My World

Communicating in this world was never easy, even in those happy days before everybody became so confused about just where "this world" begins and ends. I suppose I need hardly remind you that it is a wide world, (broadly speaking) and one which, whatever the psychological implications, is increasingly preoccupied with talking to itself. Instantaneous contact across great distances is a relatively recent phenomenon, and has had a devastating effect upon the Isolation Industry. Large numbers of disaffected hermits, forlorn lighthouse-keepers, walled-off widows, alienated adolescents, and solitary seniors have been lured back into contact with society by the temptations of telegraph, telephone, radio, and television. Never has there been a greater threat to our fundamental right to remain desperately lonely and miserable.

It cannot be denied, however, that all these advanced communication systems do have certain benefits. For example, they enable us to respond very quickly to emergency situations, such as massive power failures and transportation tie-ups—most of which would of course never happen at all if we weren't so dependent on our advanced communication systems.

But the planet we currently inhabit is, for better or worse, no longer the only world we are interested in communicating with. The era of space exploration has created vast new possibilities for being misunderstood. Those with the equipment to do so are continually shooting messages and objects into Space—but, for all our friendly intentions, Space appears to dislike being shot at. At any rate, Space has not yet replied with anything more cordial than an occasional lump of rock.

© ASHLEIGH BRILLIANT 1982.
SANTA BARBARA

POT-SHOTS NO. 2532.

# EVER SINCE
# I GOT ON THE WORLD,

I'VE WONDERED
IF
THE DRIVER
REALLY KNOWS
WHERE
WE'RE GOING.

*Ashleigh Brilliant*

Depuis que je suis monté
dans le monde, je me
suis demandé si le
conducteur savait vraiment
où nous allions.

© BRILLIANT ENTERPRISES 1976
SANTA BARBARA

POT-SHOTS NO. 885

## IF YOU WERE MAKING

### LESS **NOISE,**

*Ashleigh
Brilliant*

YOU MIGHT HEAR ME
BEGGING YOU
TO MAKE
LESS
NOISE.

Si vous faisiez
moins de bruit,
vous pourriez peut-être
m'entendre
vous supplier de faire
moins de bruit.

© ASHLEIGH BRILLIANT 1982.
SANTA BARBARA

POT-SHOTS NO. 2598.

# ISN'T IT SURPRISING
# WHAT
# TERRIBLE
# THINGS
# PEOPLE
# WILL DO,

## JUST TO
## CHANGE A LINE
## ON A MAP.

*Ashleigh Brilliant*

N'est-il pas surprenant
de voir quelles horribles
choses les gens font,
juste pour changer
une ligne sur une carte.

POT-SHOTS NO. 1392.

Ashleigh Brilliant
SANTA BARBARA

IT'S NOT CIVILIZED
FOR PEOPLE
TO KILL
EACH OTHER,

UNLESS
THEY HAVE
LEGAL PERMISSION
TO DO SO.

©ASHLEIGH BRILLIANT 1978

Il n'est pas civilisé
de se tuer les uns les autres,
à moins d'avoir
la permission légale de le faire.

©BRILLIANT ENTERPRISES 1977 POT-SHOTS NO. 1177

Ashleigh Brilliant
SANTA BARBARA

THE BEST WAY
TO STOP
THREATENING
EACH
OTHER

IS TO FIND SOMETHING
THAT THREATENS US ALL.

La meilleure façon d'arrêter
de se menacer les uns
les autres est de trouver
quelque chose
qui nous menace tous.

©ASHLEIGH BRILLIANT 1982.

POT-SHOTS NO 2570.

THE WORLD IS OPEN
TO THE PUBLIC,

Ashleigh Brilliant
SANTA BARBARA

BUT
NOBODY
EVER SEES
ENOUGH,

BEFORE
CLOSING-
TIME.

Le monde est ouvert
au public,
mais personne n'en voit
jamais assez
avant la fermeture.

Certains esprits ne
changeront jamais
jusqu'à ce qu'il y ait
assez de gens
qui veuillent risquer
leur vie pour les changer.

Les futures générations se
demanderont
pourquoi nous avons enduré
tant de malheurs que
nous avions le pouvoir
de changer.

Nous ne sommes pas
responsables pour les
actes de nos ancêtres—
alors pourquoi
devraient-ils nous
faire sentir fiers ou honteux?

**COMMITTING CRIMES** IS NOT NECESSARILY THE MOST DESIRABLE WAY OF BECOMING INVOLVED IN YOUR COMMUNITY.

POT-SHOTS NO. 5140.

© ASHLEIGH BRILLIANT 1990.

Commettre des crimes n'est pas nécessairement la façon la plus désirable de devenir engagé dans sa communauté.

POT-SHOTS NO. 2466.

NO MATTER WHAT THE WEAPONS, ALL PEOPLE WHO HAVE BEEN KILLED BY THEM ARE EQUALLY DEAD.

© ASHLEIGH BRILLIANT 1982. SANTA BARBARA

Peu importe les armes, tous les gens qui ont été tués par elles sont morts pareillement.

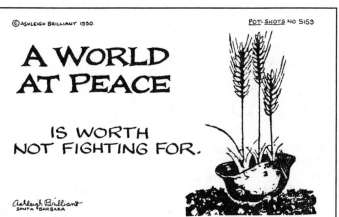

© ASHLEIGH BRILLIANT 1990.

POT-SHOTS NO 5159

**A WORLD AT PEACE** IS WORTH NOT FIGHTING FOR.

Un monde en paix vaut la peine qu'on ne se batte pas pour lui.

© ASHLEIGH BRILLIANT 1990.   POT-SHOTS NO. 5164.

# IF IT'S WAR BETWEEN MAN AND NATURE, I'M ON MAN'S SIDE~

### BUT MUST IT BE WAR?

*Ashleigh Brilliant*
SANTA BARBARA

S'il s'agit de la guerre
entre l'homme et la nature,
je suis du côté de l'homme—
mais faut-il la guerre?

© ASHLEIGH BRILLIANT 1990.   POT-SHOTS NO. 5183

# WHAT GOOD IS FREEDOM OF SPEECH,

### UNLESS THERE ARE PEOPLE WHO WILL LISTEN?

*Ashleigh Brilliant*
SANTA BARBARA

A quoi bon
la liberté d'expression,
à moins qu'il y ait des gens
qui veuillent écouter?

© ASHLEIGH BRILLIANT 1990.   POT-SHOTS NO. 5221.

# TO FIND OUT WHERE YOU ARE,

### IT IS SOMETIMES NECESSARY TO GO SOMEWHERE ELSE.

*Ashleigh Brilliant*
SANTA BARBARA

Pour trouver
où vous êtes,
il est parfois nécessaire
d'aller ailleurs.

© ASHLEIGH BRILLIANT 1991.                    POT-SHOTS NO. 5630

NATURE CLEANS UP
HER OWN MESSES ~
BUT WHY SHOULD WE EXPECT HER
TO CLEAN UP OURS?

Ashleigh Brilliant
SANTA BARBARA

La nature nettoie
sa propre saleté—
mais pourquoi devrions-nous
compter sur elle pour
nettoyer la nôtre?

© ASHLEIGH BRILLIANT 1992                    POT-SHOTS NO. 5644.

Ashleigh Brilliant
SANTA BARBARA

STOP THE
POPULATION
EXPLOSION!

THERE ARE
ALREADY
MORE PEOPLE
ON EARTH
THAN
I'LL EVER
GET TO
KNOW.

Arrêtez l'explosion
de population!
il y a déjà
sur terre plus de gens
que je ne pourrai
jamais connaître.

© ASHLEIGH BRILLIANT 1992.                    POT-SHOTS NO 5705.

IT'S EASIER TO GO
FROM SHOUTING
TO
KILLING

THAN
FROM KILLING
BACK TO
SHOUTING.

Ashleigh Brilliant
SANTA BARBARA

Il est plus facile d'aller
des cris au meurtre
que de retourner du meurtre
aux cris.

© ASHLEIGH BRILLIANT 1992.                    POT-SHOTS NO 5777

# TENSIONS ARE CONSTANTLY HIGH

## ALL ALONG THE BORDER BETWEEN RIGHT AND WRONG.

*Ashleigh Brilliant*
SANTA BARBARA

Les tensions sont
constamment hautes
le long de la frontière
entre le bien et le mal.

© ASHLEIGH BRILLIANT 1992.          POT-SHOTS NO. 5886.

# WHY SHOULD WE PUT LAND TO OTHER USES,

## WHEN ITS OBVIOUS PURPOSE IS TO ACCOMMODATE MORE CARS?

*Ashleigh
Brilliant*
SANTA
BARBARA

Pourquoi devrions-nous
utiliser la terre autrement,
quand son but évident
est de recevoir plus de
voitures?

© ASHLEIGH BRILLIANT 1992
SANTA BARBARA                    POT-SHOTS NO. 5850.

# THE NATIONAL FLAG

## ALWAYS MAKES AN EXCELLENT BLINDFOLD.

*Ashleigh
Brilliant*

Le drapeau national
fait toujours
un excellent bandeau
sur les yeux.

POT-SHOTS NO. 5899.

# I'M AFRAID WORLD PEACE MAY FINALLY COME

## ONLY WHEN NOTHING ANY LONGER SEEMS WORTH FIGHTING FOR.

*Ashleigh Brilliant SANTA BARBARA*

J'ai bien peur que
la paix mondiale
puisse finalement
arriver seulement
lorsqu'il n'y aura plus
rien pour quoi
il semble valoir la peine
de se battre.

---

POT-SHOTS NO. 5790.

# MANY WORLD PROBLEMS COULD BE SOLVED,

## IF MORE PEOPLE WOULD JUST GO AWAY AND LIVE SOMEWHERE ELSE.

*Ashleigh Brilliant SANTA BARBARA*

Beaucoup de problèmes
mondiaux
pourraient être résolus,
si simplement plus de gens
partaient
et vivaient ailleurs.

---

POT-SHOTS NO. 5953.

# WE DON'T NEED LAWS TO MAKE PEOPLE CARE MORE ABOUT EACH OTHER~

## WHAT WE NEED ARE DISASTERS.

*Ashleigh Brilliant SANTA BARBARA*

On n'a pas besoin de lois
pour que les gens se
soucient plus
les uns des autres—
on a besoin de désastres.

© ASHLEIGH BRILLIANT 1980          POT SHOTS NO 1738

WHY DOES
MOST OF THE
WORLD
LET SOME OF
THE WORLD
BEHAVE
SO BADLY
FOR
SO LONG?

*Ashleigh Brilliant
SANTA BARBARA*

Pourquoi la plupart
du monde
laisse une partie du monde
se comporter si mal
si longtemps?

© ASHLEIGH BRILLIANT 1992. SANTA BARBARA.          POT-SHOTS NO. 5987

HAVE
YOU
HAD YOUR
VIOLENCE
TODAY?

*Ashleigh Brilliant*

Avez-vous eu
votre violence
aujourd'hui?

© ASHLEIGH BRILLIANT 1992.          POT-SHOTS NO. 5968

THIS MUST HAVE BEEN
A BEAUTIFUL
PLACE,

BEFORE
EVERYBODY
CAME HERE
TO ENJOY
ITS BEAUTY.

*Ashleigh Brilliant
SANTA BARBARA*

Cela dut être
un bel endroit,
avant que tout le monde
n'y soit venu
pour goûter sa beauté.

POT-SHOTS NO 5923

MODERN
MEDICINE
MAKES ME
BELIEVE
IN PROGRESS,

BUT
MODERN ART
REVIVES
MY
DOUBTS.

©ASHLEIGH BRILLIANT 1992.

Ashleigh Brilliant
SANTA BARBARA

La médecine moderne
me fait croire au progrès,
mais l'art moderne
ravive mes doutes.

---

©ASHLEIGH BRILLIANT 1992. SANTA BARBARA

POT SHOTS NO 6030

OUR TWO PEOPLES
WILL ALWAYS
BE FRIENDS,

IF YOURS
CAN
CONTROL
THEIR
OBNOXIOUS
TENDENCIES.

Ashleigh Brilliant

Nos deux peuples
seront toujours amis,
si les vôtres peuvent
contrôler leurs tendances
désagréables.

---

©ASHLEIGH BRILLIANT 1980.

POT-SHOTS NO. 5053.

PLEASE DON'T
TELL ME
HOW THE
WORLD
WILL
END ~
I WANT
IT TO BE
A SURPRISE.

Ashleigh Brilliant
SANTA BARBARA

S'il vous plaît, ne me
racontez pas
comment le monde va finir—
je veux que cela soit
une surprise.

BY **ASHLEIGH BRILLIANT**

**Pot-Shots** ®

POT-SHOTS NO. 5368.

ON THIS GREAT VOYAGE OF LIFE,

WHY DO I SO OFTEN FEEL LIKE A STOWAWAY?

Ashleigh Brilliant
SANTA BARBARA

Dans cette grande
traversée de la vie,
pourquoi est-ce que
si souvent je me
sens comme un passager
clandestin?

# VIII. Life Lines

Let's talk about Life—because so much of Life is about talk. From baby's first words to the very last words of whomever baby ultimately becomes, being alive usually means having something to say, even if we don't all have a gift for saying it well, or the best opportunities for saying it at all. When this curious need to communicate has no other chance to surface, it finds fulfillment in our dreams—those strange messages we keep sending ourselves in the secret hours of the night.

Writing is of course another form of talking, and I personally am one of those endowed, or afflicted, with the tendency to feel more alive when writing than at almost any other time. But feeling alive, as we all know only too well, doesn't necessarily mean feeling happy, and the thoughts on the following pages may not help to boost living as an activity on any of the popularity charts.

Still, living—and writing—do have their exalted moments. For example, there is always the chance that some reader may find something I say to be of real personal value. According to the letters I receive, this actually does happen now and then. But—just my luck—it turns out, with dismaying frequency, to be only because the grateful reader has completely misinterpreted what I said.

© ASHLEIGH BRILLIANT 1973    POT-SHOTS NO. 1503

# LIFE IS SURELY WORTH A CERTAIN AMOUNT OF STRUGGLE,

## BUT SOMETIMES I WONDER, EXACTLY HOW MUCH?

La vie vaut sûrement
une certaine quantité
de lutte,
mais parfois je me
demande
exactement combien?

POT-SHOTS NO. 1430.

Ashleigh
Brilliant
SANTA
BARBARA

# WHY ARE MY REHEARSALS ALWAYS SO MUCH BETTER THAN MY PERFORMANCES?

© ASHLEIGH BRILLIANT 1973

Pourquoi
mes répétitions sont-elles
toujours largement
meilleures
que mes performances?

POT-SHOTS NO. 1489.

Ashleigh
Brilliant
SANTA
BARBARA

# SOME PEOPLE SPEND ALL OF LIFE WORRYING ABOUT THE DESTINATION —

## OTHERS SIMPLY TRY TO ENJOY THE JOURNEY.

Certaines personnes
passent toute
leur vie a s'inquiéter
de leur destination—
d'autres essaient
simplement d'apprécier
le voyage.

© ASHLEIGH BRILLIANT 1973

© ASHLEIGH BRILLIANT 1980.
SANTA BARBARA

POT-SHOTS NO. 1823.

**IF YOU WANT TO SPEND TOMORROW BEING GLAD YOU DID IT,**

**YOU HAVE TO DO IT TODAY.**

Si vous voulez passer le lendemain à être content de l'avoir fait, vous devez le faire aujourd'hui.

© ASHLEIGH BRILLIANT 1980
SANTA BARBARA

POT-SHOTS NO. 1836.

**CONGRATULATE ME! I'VE GRADUATED TO A NEW LEVEL OF SUFFERING.**

Félicitez-moi! J'ai gradué à un niveau supérieur de souffrance.

© ASHLEIGH BRILLIANT 1980.

POT-SHOTS NO. 1960.

Ashleigh Brilliant SANTA BARBARA

**MY LIFE IS ALREADY COMPLICATED ENOUGH,**

**WITHOUT TRYING TO INTRODUCE ORGANIZATION INTO IT.**

Ma vie est déjà suffisamment compliquée sans qu'on essaie d'y mettre de l'ordre.

POT-SHOTS NO 2027.

For me,
the
easy
things
are so
difficult,
I never
have
time to
attempt
the hard ones.

©ASHLEIGH BRILLIANT 1980

Pour moi, les choses faciles
sont si difficiles
que je n'ai jamais le temps
de tenter les choses difficiles.

©ASHLEIGH BRILLIANT 1982

POT-SHOTS NO. 2376.

Why
is the place
where I want to be

so often
so far
from
where
I am?

Pourquoi est-ce que l'endroit
où je veux être
si souvent est si loin de
là où je me trouve?

©ASHLEIGH BRILLIANT 1982. SANTA BARBARA

POT-SHOTS NO. 2571.

I'LL FACE
THE PROBLEM
OF HOW
TO LIVE

WHEN
I COME
TO IT.

Je confronterai le problème
de savoir comment vivre
quand je l'aborder.

© ASHLEIGH BRILLIANT 1983.
SANTA BARBARA

POT-SHOTS NO. 2874.

**I'M WILLING TO COME TO TERMS WITH LIFE,**

IF WE CAN MEET ON NEUTRAL GROUND.

Ashleigh Brilliant

Je veux bien
m'arranger avec ma vie,
si nous pouvons nous
rencontrer
sur un terrain neutre.

© ASHLEIGH BRILLIANT 1987.

POT-SHOTS NO. 4027.

**IT'S SURPRISING HOW FAR YOU CAN GO THROUGH LIFE**

WITHOUT EVER HAVING WHAT YOU REALLY NEED.

Ashleigh Brilliant
SANTA BARBARA

Il est surprenant de voir
jusqu'où on peut
aller dans la vie,
sans jamais avoir
ce dont on a
réellement besoin.

© ASHLEIGH BRILLIANT 1990.
SANTA BARBARA

POT-SHOTS NO 5065

**WE CAN'T ALL BE WINNERS,**

BUT WE CAN ALL BE TRYERS.

Ashleigh Brilliant

On ne peut pas tous
être vainqueurs,
mais on peut tous
être essayeurs.

© ASHLEIGH BRILLIANT 1983.
SANTA BARBARA

POT-SHOTS NO. 2846.

*Ashleigh
Brilliant*

# IT TAKES
# COURAGE
# TO FACE LIFE,

### BUT
### IT ALSO
### TAKES COURAGE
### TO REFUSE TO FACE IT.

Cela demande du courage
d'affronter la vie,
mais cela demande aussi
du courage de refuser
de l'affronter.

---

© ASHLEIGH BRILLIANT 1990.

POT-SHOTS NO. 5253.

# HOW CAN I
# BE SURE
that
staying alive
is really
to my advantage?

*Ashleigh Brilliant*
SANTA BARBARA

Comment puis-je être
sûr que rester
en vie est vraiment
à mon avantage?

---

WHY DOES
LIFE KEEP
TEACHING
ME

© ASHLEIGH BRILLIANT 1990.

POT-SHOTS NO. 5066

*Ashleigh
Brilliant*
SANTA BARBARA

LESSONS
I HAVE
NO DESIRE
TO LEARN?

Pourquoi la vie
continue-t-elle
à m'enseigner des
leçons que je n'ai
aucun désir d'apprendre?

© ASHLEIGH BRILLIANT 1990.  POT-SHOTS NO. 5144.

# TRYING IS EXTREMELY IMPORTANT,

BUT WHAT'S EVEN MORE IMPORTANT IS: SUCCEEDING.

*Ashleigh Brilliant*
SANTA BARBARA

Essayer est extrêmement important, mais ce qui est encore plus important est: réussir.

---

© ASHLEIGH BRILLIANT 1990.  POT-SHOTS NO. 5152.

# IF YOU CAN NEITHER ACCEPT IT NOR CHANGE IT,

TRY TO LAUGH AT IT.

*Ashleigh Brilliant*
SANTA BARBARA

Si vous ne pouvez ni l'accepter ni le changer, essayez d'en rire.

---

© ASHLEIGH BRILLIANT 1991.  POT-SHOTS NO. 5330.

# WHICH IS MORE SAD:

TO LOSE YOUR HEART'S DESIRE,

OR TO FIND IT NO LONGER DESIRABLE?

*Ashleigh Brilliant*
SANTA BARBARA

Qu'est-ce qui est le plus triste: de perdre le désir de votre coeur, ou de ne plus le trouver désirable?

POT-SHOTS NO 5374  ©ASHLEIGH BRILLIANT 1991.

## I SEE WHAT LIFE IS ~

### AND YET, LIKE A FOOL, I STILL GO ON LIVING IT.

*Ashleigh Brilliant*
SANTA BARBARA

Je vois ce qu'est la vie—
et pourtant, comme un idiot,
je continue à la vivre.

©ASHLEIGH BRILLIANT 1990.

POT-SHOTS NO. 5170.

*Ashleigh Brilliant*
SANTA BARBARA

## STAY ALIVE!

### IT'S THE LEAST YOU CAN DO.

Restez en vie! C'est
la moindre des choses
que vous puissiez faire.

©ASHLEIGH BRILLIANT 1992.

POT-SHOTS NO. 5770.

## MORNINGS ARE WONDERFUL ~

### BUT WHY MUST THEY SO OFTEN BE FOLLOWED BY THE REST OF THE DAY?

*Ashleigh Brilliant*
SANTA BARBARA

Les matins sont merveilleux—
mais pourquoi doivent-ils
être si souvent suivis par
le reste de la journée?

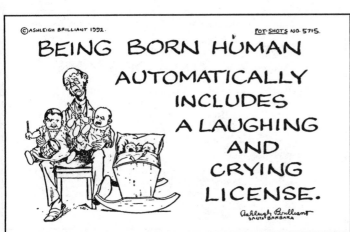

© ASHLEIGH BRILLIANT 1992.  POT-SHOTS NO 5651.

# I CAN TAKE REALITY IN SMALL DOSES ~

Ashleigh Brilliant
SANTA BARBARA

BUT LIFE IS MUCH TOO BIG A DOSE.

Je peux supporter la réalité
à petites doses—
mais la vie est une dose
beaucoup trop forte.

© ASHLEIGH BRILLIANT 1992.  POT-SHOTS NO. 5715.

# BEING BORN HUMAN AUTOMATICALLY INCLUDES A LAUGHING AND CRYING LICENSE.

Ashleigh Brilliant
SANTA BARBARA

Etre né humain
implique automatiquement
un permis de rire et de pleurer.

© ASHLEIGH BRILLIANT 1991.  POT-SHOTS NO 5545.

Ashleigh
Brilliant
SANTA
BARBARA

# I LIKE IT HERE IN THIS PART OF MY LIFE ~

WHY MUST I TRAVEL ON?

Je l'aime bien ici
dans cette partie de ma vie—
pourquoi dois-je
continuer à voyager?

© ASHLEIGH BRILLIANT 1992.    POT-SHOTS NO. 5787.

# LIFE NEED NOT BE A STRUGGLE ~

## IT CAN BE A SIMPLE DOWNWARD SLIDE.

Ashleigh Brilliant
SANTA BARBARA

La vie n'a pas besoin d'être une lutte—
elle peut être
un simple glissement
vers le bas.

© ASHLEIGH BRILLIANT 1992. SANTA BARBARA.    POT-SHOTS NO. 6010.

# NOW THAT I SEE WHAT KIND OF GAME LIFE IS,

## I'M NOT SURE I WANT TO PLAY.

Ashleigh Brilliant

Maintenant que je vois
quel genre de jeu est la vie,
je ne suis pas sûr
que je veuille jouer.

© ASHLEIGH BRILLIANT 1992. SANTA BARBARA.    POT-SHOTS NO. 6023.

# LIFE IS A WONDERFUL OPPORTUNITY ~

## I WISH IT HAD COME WHEN I WAS MORE READY FOR IT.

Ashleigh Brilliant

La vie est
une merveilleuse
opportunité—
j' aurais bien aimé
qu'elle arrive
quand je m'y étais
mieux préparé.

**EVERY TIME I DO WHAT I HAVE TO DO,**

**I GET A LITTLE FARTHER INTO TROUBLE.**

© ASHLEIGH BRILLIANT 1992. SANTA BARBARA — POT-SHOTS NO. 5854

Chaque fois que je fais
ce que j'ai à faire,
je m'attire de plus en plus
d'ennuis.

**LIFE ISN'T EASY ~**

**SOMETIMES IT'S ALL I CAN DO TO STAY UNCONSCIOUS.**

© ASHLEIGH BRILLIANT 1992. SANTA BARBARA — POT-SHOTS NO. 5981.

La vie n'est pas facile—
parfois c'est tout ce que
je peux faire
pour rester inconscient.

**EVERYBODY NEEDS TWO LIFETIMES:**

**ONE TO SEE WHAT THERE IS, ANOTHER TO COME BACK TO THE BEST.**

© ASHLEIGH BRILLIANT 1981. Ashleigh Brilliant SANTA BARBARA — POT-SHOTS NO. 2270.

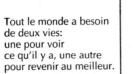

Tout le monde a besoin
de deux vies:
une pour voir
ce qu'il y a, une autre
pour revenir au meilleur.

# Pot-Shots

### BY ASHLEIGH BRILLIANT

© ASHLEIGH BRILLIANT 1990.

POT-SHOTS NO. 5061.

**BUT IF WE ELIMINATE TOO MANY UNNECESSARY REGULATIONS,**

**TOO MANY PEOPLE MAY LOSE THEIR JOBS.**

Aber wenn wir zu viel unnötige Vorschriften abschaffen, werden zu viele Leute arbeitslos.

# IX. Fool Employment

We will now attempt to focus our thoughts upon Working (which is often much easier that actually doing any work.) It seems ironic that, when our goal as a society has for centuries been to eliminate the need to labor, a chief concern of many people today is to find work—or, if already blessed with a job, to keep it.

To add to the irony, since most modern employment no longer provides the physical exercise which our old-fashioned bodies still require, people who don't get enough real work to do at work now have to take special time for it, and even sometimes pay for it, outside of work.

Indeed, the hardest work actually available in the modern workplace may be that of dealing with the problem of how to communicate. Failure to do so effectively is an occupational hazard whose consequences (depending on the occupation) can range from losing a box of paper-clips to losing Western Europe.

Such catastrophes would, of course, be less likely if people could only follow directions—or give directions capable of being followed—or simply think for themselves, without needing to be directed at all. But when things become *that* simple, there'll be no need for such Brilliant Thoughts® as the following, and I myself will be out of a job.

© BRILLIANT ENTERPRISES 1977.
SANTA BARBARA

POT-SHOTS NO. 1049.

# I'M NEW HERE —

## WHO SHOULD I PROSTRATE MYSELF IN FRONT OF?

*Ashleigh Brilliant*

Ich bin neu hier—
wem soll ich mich
zu Füssen werfen?

© BRILLIANT ENTERPRISES 1974.
SANTA BARBARA

*Ashleigh Brilliant*

POT-SHOTS NO. 613.

## THE BEST WAY TO
## ADVERTISE
## IS SIMPLY TO BE
## UNUSUALLY GOOD.

Die beste
Werbung
ist ganz einfach
hervorragend zu sein.

POT-SHOTS NO. 2193

IT WAS ONLY
YESTERDAY'S SACRIFICES
THAT MADE POSSIBLE
TODAY'S DISAPPOINTMENTS.

© ASHLEIGH BRILLIANT 381 SANTA BARBARA

*Ashleigh Brilliant*

Nur durch die Opfer
von gestern
sind die Enttäuschungen
von heute möglich

POT-SHOTS NO. 2578.

MOST OF US
LIVE IN
SAFETY,

ONLY
BECAUSE
SOME OF US
ARE ALWAYS
WILLING
TO FACE
DANGER.

© ASHLEIGH BRILLIANT 1982. SANTA BARBARA

*Ashleigh Brilliant*

Der grösste Teil von uns
lebt in Sicherheit,
weil sich einige von uns
ständig Gefahren aussetzen.

© ASHLEIGH BRILLIANT 1988. SANTA BARBARA.

POT-SHOTS NO. 4474.

ALWAYS
FOLLOW
ORDERS,

UNLESS THEY ARE
OBVIOUSLY
CRAZY OR ILLEGAL,

OR YOU HAVE
A BETTER IDEA.

*Ashleigh Brilliant*

Befehle sind stets zu
befolgen, es sei denn sie
sind offenbar verückt,
illegal, oder Sie haben
eine bessere Idee.

© ASHLEIGH BRILLIANT 1983
SANTA BARBARA

POT-SHOTS NO 2763
*Ashleigh Brilliant*

BE A TOURIST!
HARD WORK, NO PAY,
UNCERTAIN CONDITIONS,
AND LONG PERIODS AWAY FROM HOME.

Werden Sie Tourist:
Schwerarbeit, keine
Bezahlung, unsichere
Bedingungen, lange
Abwesenheiten von
zu Hause!

*Fool Employment  121*

© ASHLEIGH BRILLIANT 1988.
SANTA BARBARA

POT-SHOTS NO. 4663.

ANYBODY WHO
REQUIRES
MY SIGNATURE
ON ANY
LEGAL
DOCUMENT

OBVIOUSLY
DOESN'T
TRUST ME.

Ashleigh Brilliant

Wenn man von mir verlangt
ein amtliches Schriftstück
zu unterzeichnen, wird mir
klar, dass man mir
nicht traut.

POT-SHOTS NO. 5151.

Will I ever
become
successful
enough
to be
investigated
by a
government agency?

© ASHLEIGH BRILLIANT 1990.

Ashleigh Brilliant
SANTA BARBARA

Werde ich je so viel Erfolg
haben, dass mich die
Behörden dass mich die
untersuchen?

© ASHLEIGH BRILLIANT 1990.

POT-SHOTS NO. 5172.

EVERY DAY
MILLIONS OF INNOCENT PEOPLE
ARE FORCED FROM THEIR HOMES

BY A DISASTER
CALLED "WORK."

Ashleigh Brilliant
SANTA BARBARA

Tagtäglich werden Millionen
unschuldige Menschen
gezwungen ihr Heim
zu verlassen wegen der
Katastrophe, die sich
"Arbeit" nennt.

Nichts zeugt mehr von
ehrlicher Absicht
als Vorauszahlung in bar.

Das Wichtigste ist nicht,
das Problem zu lösen, sondern
jemandem die Schuld
zuzuschieben.

Auf Ratschlag
unserer Kundschaft,
gedenken wir
unseren Betrieb zu schliessen.

Manchmal verlieren Leute
ihr Leben,
Nur dass andere Leute
ihr Geld nicht verlieren.

Ich brauche immer länger
etwas zu beenden,
wenn ich keinen blassen
Dunst habe, was ich
eigentlich tue.

Was es heisst
"der Beste" zu sein,
kommt ganz darauf an
wie gut die anderen sind.

POT-SHOTS NO 5690

**What I need
is
a job I can
get
without ever
having to
make a good
impression.**

Ashleigh Brilliant
SANTA BARBARA

Was ich brauche,
ist ein Stelle, die ich kriege
ohne einen guten Eindruck
zu machen.

---

POT-SHOTS NO. 5851.

Ashleigh Brilliant
SANTA BARBARA

**FIRST GOD MADE
BUSINESSES,**

**BUT THE
BUSINESS
PEOPLE
WERE
LONELY
AND UNHAPPY,**

**SO THEN
GOD CREATED
CUSTOMERS.**

Am ersten Tag erschuf Gott
die Geschäfte, aber die
Geschäftsleute waren einsam
und unglücklich, deshalb
erschuf Gott am zweiten
Tag die Kunden.

---

POT-SHOTS NO. 5955.

**ON YOUR WAY TO SUCCESS,**

**REMEMBER
TO
ALLOW
PLENTY
OF TIME
FOR
DELAYS
IN
TRAFFIC.**

Auf Ihrem Weg zum Erfolg,
denken sie daran
viel Zeit
für Verkehrsstau ein
zuberechnen.

Ich weiss genau,
wie lange ich brauchen
werde: die zur Verfügung
stehende Zeit,
zuzüglich etwas länger.

Ihr geringfügiges Problem
erhält selbstverständlich
die passende
Aufmerksamkeit von
unserem überarbeiteten
Personal.

Was einen Profi
von einem Amateur
unterscheidet:
dem Profi braucht
die Sache keinen Spass
zu machen.

*126*

© ASHLEIGH BRILLIANT 1992.  POT-SHOTS NO. 5975.

# YOU TOO

## CAN BE EXPLOITED AND CHEATED IN YOUR SPARE TIME.

*Ashleigh Brilliant*
SANTA BARBARA

Auch Sie
können sich in Ihrer Freizeit
ausbeuten und betrügen
lassen.

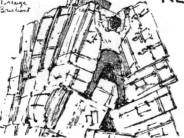

© BRILLIANT ENTERPRISES 1977
SANTA BARBARA

POT-SHOTS NO. 384

## ACCORDING TO OUR CAREFULLY-KEPT RECORDS,

### ALL OUR AFFAIRS ARE IN TOTAL CONFUSION.

Laut unseren
gewissenhaft geführten
Büchern, befinden sich alle
unsere Geschäfte
in vollkommenem Chaos.

© ASHLEIGH BRILLIANT 1980. SANTA BARBARA.  POT-SHOTS NO. 1996.

# I'M ALWAYS PUNCTUAL,

## WHEN THE TIME COMES TO STOP WORK.

*Ashleigh Brilliant*

Ich bin immer pünktlich
wenn's Zeit ist
zum Arbeitsschluss.

**Pot-Shots** BY ASHLEIGH BRILLIANT

POT-SHOTS NO. 5019.

I WON'T
LET GO
OF THE PAST,

UNTIL
YOU PROVE
I'LL NEVER
NEED IT
IN
THE
FUTURE.

*Ashleigh Brilliant*

Ich werde erst
von der Vergangenheit
ablassen, wenn du mir
beweist, dass ich
sie nicht für die Zukunft
brauche.

# X. Time Capsules

That elusive entity called Time, whom we visit here, is no friend of Communication, and in fact loves to set up obstacles between people. It is Time who deteriorates our roads and bridges, delays information until it is out of date, and causes us, when we are at last ready and able to communicate, to forget what it was we wanted to say.

Among his (or her?) other tricks, Time makes words change their meanings, and causes whole languages to decline and perish, sometimes leaving behind writings which nobody can read or understand. That may indeed be the fate of this very book. But don't let it trouble you. Languages are only vehicles for thoughts, and these Thoughts were built to last.

Even now, as one of the compensations of my own bruising encounter with Time, (mercifully, there are some!) I enjoy the frequent satisfaction of being excitedly discovered by people who were not even alive when my encapsulated wisdoms first appeared in print. Surely this literary longevity (together with the fact that I am, after all, a Doctor of Philosophy) entitles me to offer my own prescription for your current condition. So here it is: take a few time capsules, and call me in the next chapter.

Das Leben is zu kurz,
um alles zu tun,
aber zu lang
um nichts zu tun.

Ich tue was ich kann,
die Ankunft meiner
Geburtstage zu verzögern,
aber kein Mittel scheint
zu helfen.

Zum Kampf gegen das
Fortschreiten der Zeit habe
ich zwei Waffen:
das Gedächtnis und die
Hoffnung.

© ASHLEIGH BRILLIANT 1985. SANTA BARBARA.   POT-SHOTS NO-3723.

To save time,
I'm
considering
declaring
the rest
of my life
a total
failure
in advance.

*Ashleigh Brilliant*

Aus Gründen der
Zeitersparnis, bedenke
ich schon im Voraus
den Rest meines lebens als
kompletter Fehlschlag
zu erklären.

---

© ASHLEIGH BRILLIANT 1990.   POT-SHOTS NO. 5185.

WHY
MUST WE
KEEP LOOKING
FORWARD,
WHEN
THE VIEW
IN THE OTHER
DIRECTION
IS BECOMING
INCREASINGLY
PLEASANT?

*Ashleigh Brilliant*
SANTA BARBARA

Warum immer nur in die
Zukunft blicken, wenn
der Blick in die andere
Richtung mehr und mehr
angenehm wird?

---

© ASHLEIGH BRILLIANT 1990.   *Ashleigh Brilliant* SANTA BARBARA   POT-SHOTS NO 5293

I'M
NO LONGER
CAPABLE
OF DOING
CERTAIN
THINGS,
BUT SOME OF THEM
(HAPPILY)
WERE BAD THINGS.

Zu manchen Taten
bin ich nicht mehr fähig,
aber Gottseidank
waren da Untaten dabei.

© ASHLEIGH BRILLIANT 1991
POT-SHOTS NO. 5370.

## IF EACH PERSON COULD SAVE JUST ONE SECOND,

### THE WHOLE WORLD COULD SAVE HUNDREDS OF YEARS!

Ashleigh Brilliant
SANTA BARBARA

Wenn jeder Mensch
nur eine Sekunde einsparen
könnte, würde die ganze
Welt Jahrhunderte
sparen.

© ASHLEIGH BRILLIANT 1991.
POT-SHOTS NO. 5398.

## IT'S NOT EASY TO FIND YOURSELF SLOWING DOWN

### IN A WORLD THAT'S SPEEDING UP.

Ashleigh Brilliant
SANTA BARBARA

Es ist nicht leicht zu merken
dass man langsamer wird,
auf einer Welt die sich
beschleunigt.

© ASHLEIGH BRILLIANT 1991.
POT-SHOTS NO 5453

Ashleigh
Brilliant
SANTA BARBARA

## I CAN'T BELIEVE IT'S BEEN A WHOLE YEAR

### SINCE WHATEVER HAPPENED A YEAR AGO.

Ich kann es kaum glauben:
Es ist ein ganzes Jahr her
seit was auch immer
vor einem Jahr geschehen ist.

© ASHLEIGH BRILLIANT 1991    POT-SHOTS NO 5485

The best ways of passing time

are those that help you to forget that time is passing.

Ashleigh Brilliant SANTA BARBARA

Der beste Zeitvertreib
ist derjenige,
der mir hilft, zu vergessen,
dass die Zeit vergeht.

© ASHLEIGH BRILLIANT 1991.    POT-SHOTS NO. 5487.

THE FARTHER I GO INTO THE FUTURE,

THE MORE OF MYSELF I LEAVE BEHIND.

Ashleigh Brilliant
SANTA BARBARA

Je weiter ich
in die Zukunft schreite,
desto mehr lasse ich von mir
selbst hinter mir.

© ASHLEIGH BRILLIANT 1991    POT-SHOTS NO 5551

THE MEMORY OF A HAPPINESS

CAN LAST MUCH LONGER THAN THE HAPPINESS ITSELF.

Ashleigh Brilliant SANTA BARBARA

Die Erinnerung
an glückliche Zeiten
kann länger halten
als das Glück selbst.

© ASHLEIGH BRILLIANT 1991

POT-SHOTS NO. 5499

## GIVEN ENOUGH TIME, I CAN ADJUST TO ANYTHING,

Ashleigh Brilliant
SANTA BARBARA

but I've never yet been given enough time.

Wenn man mir genug Zeit
lässt, kann ich mich
an alles gewöhnen,
nur lässt man mir eben
nie genug Zeit.

© ASHLEIGH BRILLIANT 1992.

POT-SHOTS NO. 5939.

## I REFUSE TO REVEAL MY AGE,

### BUT WILL GIVE YOU A HINT ~

IT'S IN DOUBLE DIGITS.

Ashleigh Brilliant
SANTA BARBARA

Ich weigere mich,
mein Alter anzugeben,
aber hier ist ein Hinweis:
es schreibt sich mit zwei
Ziffern.

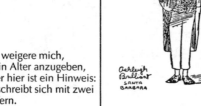

© ASHLEIGH BRILLIANT 1992.

POT-SHOTS NO. 5672.

## HOW YOU FEEL ABOUT GETTING OLDER

Ashleigh Brilliant
SANTA BARBARA

DEPENDS LARGELY UPON HOW LONG YOU'VE BEEN DOING IT.

Wie man sich beim
Älterwerden fült,
hängt ganz davon ab, wie
lange man dieser
Beschäftigung schon nachgeht.

© ASHLEIGH BRILLIANT 1992

POT-SHOTS NO. 6085.

**YESTERDAY HAS NOT BEEN DESTROYED, BUT IS NO LONGER ACCESSIBLE BY ORDINARY MEANS OF COMMUNICATION.**

Ashleigh Brilliant
SANTA BARBARA

Die Vergangenheit ist nicht zerstört worden, aber sie ist lediglich mit herkömmlichen Kommunikationsmitteln nicht mehr zu erreichen.

© ASHLEIGH BRILLIANT 1980
SANTA BARBARA

POT-SHOTS NO. 2009.

**A CALENDAR IS A STRANGE KIND OF CLOCK, WHICH SOMEHOW GAINS 24 HOURS EVERY DAY.**

Ashleigh Brilliant

Ein Kalender ist eine merkwürdige Art von Uhr, die irgendwie jeden Tag 24 Stunden gewinnt.

POT-SHOTS NO. 922.

**Do I remember it so clearly from a story or a dream, or from my real life?**

© BRILLIANT ENTERPRISES 1976.

Ashleigh Brilliant
SANTA BARBARA

Ich kann mich deutlich daran erinnern: aber, war es eine Geschichte, ein Traum, oder ist es wirklich passiert?

POT-SHOTS NO. 1449.

Nothing we can do can change the Past

*Ashleigh Brilliant SANTA BARBARA*

but everything we do changes the Future.

© ASHLEIGH BRILLIANT 1978.

An der Vergangenheit können wir nichts ändern, aber alles was wir tun, ändert die Zukunft.

Ich habe etwas aus der Vergangenheit mitgebracht: eine seltsame Sache names ''Erinnerung.''

© ASHLEIGH BRILLIANT 1979 SANTA BARBARA

POT-SHOTS NO 1402

I brought something with me from the past —

a strange thing called "memory."

*Ashleigh Brilliant*

POT-SHOTS NO. 4669.

FOR WHAT CRIME

IS OLD AGE THE PUNISHMENT?

© ASHLEIGH BRILLIANT 1988.

*Ashleigh Brilliant SANTA BARBARA*

Für welches Verbrechen ist das Alter die Strafe?

© ASHLEIGH BRILLIANT 1981    POT-SHOTS NO. 2318.

Ashleigh Brilliant SANTA BARBARA

# WHY DOES LIFE SEEM SO SHORT,

WHEN IT'S ACTUALLY THE LONGEST THING ANYBODY EVER GOES THROUGH?

Warum kommt einem das Leben so kurz vor? Es ist doch die langwierigste Sache, die man erlebt.

© ASHLEIGH BRILLIANT 1991.    POT-SHOTS NO. 5518.

# AS YOU GROW OLDER,

"NEVER" DOESN'T SEEM SUCH A LONG TIME.

Ashleigh Brilliant SANTA BARBARA

Wenn man älter wird, scheint "nie" nicht so lange zu sein.

POT-SHOTS NO. 2680.

# KEEP SOME SOUVENIRS OF YOUR PAST,

Ashleigh Brilliant SANTA BARBARA

OR HOW WILL YOU EVER PROVE IT WASN'T ALL A DREAM?

© ASHLEIGH BRILLIANT 1982.

Behalte einige Andenken aus deiner Vergangenheit. Wie sollteste Du sonst beweisen, dass nicht alles nur ein Traum war?

© ASHLEIGH BRILLIANT 1983.
SANTA BARBARA

POT-SHOTS NO 2744.

**THERE'S ALWAYS TIME
FOR YOU IN MY HEART,**

**IF NOT
ON MY
CALENDAR.**

*Ashleigh
Brilliant*

In meinem Herzen is immer
Zeit für Dich da, wenn
auch vielleicht nicht
auf meinem Terminkalender.

© ASHLEIGH BRILLIANT 1992. SANTA BARBARA.

POT-SHOTS NO. 6001.

**HOW DIFFERENT CAN
THINGS
GET,**

**BEFORE
THEY
COME AROUND
TO BEING
THE SAME
AGAIN?**

*Ashleigh
Brilliant*

Wie anders
können die Dinge werden
bevor sie wieder anfangen
sich zu gleichen?

© ASHLEIGH BRILLIANT 1990.

POT-SHOTS NO. 5184.

**TEARS
CAN'T
WASH OUT
THE PAST,**

**BUT
THEY CAN
SOMETIMES
HELP
SOFTEN IT
A LITTLE.**

*Ashleigh Brilliant*
SANTA BARBARA

Tränen können die
Vergangenheit nicht
ungeschehen machen,
aber sie helfen manchmal,
sie leichter zu ertragen

© ASHLEIGH BRILLIANT 1982.
SANTA BARBARA

POT-SHOTS NO. 2499.

NO WONDER
I'M WEARY!

I'VE HAD
TO SPEND
MY ENTIRE
LIFE
JUST
GETTING TO
THIS
MOMENT.

*Ashleigh Brilliant*

Kein Wunder dass ich so schlapp bin! Ich habe mein ganzes Leben gebraucht, an diesen Punkt zu kommen.

POT-SHOTS NO. 919.

# WHERE HAS
# ALL THE TIME GONE?

AND WHY DIDN'T I
SPEND MORE OF IT
WITH YOU?

© BRILLIANT ENTERPRISES 1976

*Ashleigh Brilliant*
SANTA BARBARA

Wo ist bloss die ganze Zeit hin? Und warum habe ich nicht mehr davon mit Dir verbracht?

© ASHLEIGH BRILLIANT 1992.

POT-SHOTS NO. 5737.

I'M GLAD
THE FUTURE
HASN'T COME YET,

BECAUSE
I DON'T THINK
I COULD
HANDLE IT
RIGHT NOW.

*Ashleigh Brilliant*
SANTA BARBARA

Ich bin froh, dass die Zukunft noch nicht hier ist— Ich glaube, ich könnte mich jetzt nicht mit ihr befassen.

*Time Capsules 139*

**THERE IS NO LAW AGAINST INSANITY~**

IF THERE WERE, THE ENTIRE GOVERNMENT MIGHT HAVE TO SHUT DOWN.

© ASHLEIGH BRILLIANT 1991.

POT-SHOTS NO. 5343.

Ashleigh Brilliant
SANTA BARBARA

Es gibt kein Verbot gegen Wahnsinn—denn wenn es eins gäbe, müsste die gesamte Regierung ab treten.

# XI. Mixed Signals

In an orderly universe, there should always be a place for disorderly thoughts. And any book of Brilliant Thoughts®, no matter how well organized, usually needs a chapter for those of that highly select variety known as Miscellaneous. This is it.

Lest we forget, however, that *Communication* is the theme of this whole volume, allow me to parade before you here nine of my most inspired utterances on that subject, never before assembled on a single page:

#262. INFORM ALL THE TROOPS THAT COMMUNICATIONS HAVE COMPLETELY BROKEN DOWN.

#377. I'M SORRY FOR NOT COMMUNICATING, BUT SOMETIMES IT'S VERY HARD TO WRITE ON A MOVING PLANET.

#500. I WAITED AND WAITED, AND, WHEN NO MESSAGE CAME, I KNEW IT MUST BE FROM YOU.

#840. WORDS CAN NEVER EXPRESS WHAT WORDS CAN NEVER EXPRESS.

#1085. MY SOURCES ARE UNRELIABLE, BUT THEIR INFORMATION IS FASCINATING.

#1529. WORDS ARE A WONDERFUL FORM OF COMMUNICATION—BUT THEY WILL NEVER REPLACE KISSES AND PUNCHES.

#2308. BUT IT'S ONLY WHEN I MISUNDERSTAND YOU THAT I EVER REALLY AGREE WITH YOU!

#4126. I UNDERSTOOD MOST OF YOUR MESSAGE,—BUT WOULD YOU MIND REPEATING THE LAST SCREAM?

#4339. THE FIRST EXPRESSION TO LEARN IN ANY FOREIGN LANGUAGE IS: "I'M SORRY, I DON'T SPEAK YOUR LANGUAGE."

© BRILLIANT ENTERPRISES 1977.   *Ashleigh Brilliant*   POT-SHOTS NO. 1150.
SANTA BARBARA

## IN ORDER TO DISCOVER
## WHO YOU ARE,
## FIRST LEARN
## WHO EVERYBODY ELSE IS,
## —AND YOU'RE WHAT'S LEFT.

Um Dich selbst
zu entdecken, erforsche erst
was andere sind—
was übrig bleibt, bist Du.

© ASHLEIGH BRILLIANT 1969   POT-SHOTS NO. 130
SANTA BARBARA

### I DISAGREE
### WITH WHAT YOU SAY,
### BUT I RESPECT YOUR RIGHT
### TO BE PUNISHED FOR SAYING IT.

*Ashleigh Brilliant*

Ich bin
anderer Meinung,
aber ich respektiere ihr
Recht für Ihre Meinung
bestraft zu werden.

POT-SHOTS NO. 1138.

## TOO MUCH OF ANYTHING
## CAN BE HARMFUL,

*Ashleigh Brilliant*
SANTA BARBARA

## BUT SO CAN NOT ENOUGH.

© BRILLIANT ENTERPRISES 1977.

Zuviel von allem kann
kann schädlich sein,
aber zuwenig auch.

© ASHLEIGH BRILLIANT 1975
SANTA BARBARA

POT SHOTS NO 1548

I DON'T WANT ANYTHING
TO WHICH
I AM NOT ENTITLED

BY THE
LAW OF
THE
JUNGLE.

Ich will nichts ausser
was mir nach dem
Faustrecht zusteht.

© ASHLEIGH BRILLIANT 1972
SANTA BARBARA

POT-SHOTS NO. 377

I'M SORRY
FOR NOT COMMUNICATING
BUT SOMETIMES
IT'S VERY HARD TO WRITE
ON A MOVING PLANET.

Tut mir leid, dass ich
Deinen Brief noch nicht
beantwortet habe.
Es ist manchmal schwer,
aur einem Planeten
zu schreiben, der sich
in Bewegung befindet.

POT-SHOTS NO. 1980.

I'M
WORRIED
ABOUT YOU,

BUT PLEASE
DON'T LET THAT
WORRY YOU.

© ASHLEIGH BRILLIANT 1980.

Ich mache mir Sorgen
um Dich, aber das soll
Dir bitte keine
Sorgen machen.

POT-SHOTS NO 1417.

THANKS TO
ALL THE
PIONEERS,

THERE ARE NOW
FAR TOO MANY PATHWAYS.

© ASHLEIGH BRILLIANT 1979

Dank all der Pioniere
gibt es hier jetzt
viel zu viele Pfade.

POT-SHOTS NO. 890.

WHY
HAS IT TAKEN ME
SO LONG TO TELL YOU

THAT
I FIND IT HARD
TO COMMUNICATE?

© BRILLIANT ENTERPRISES 1976.

Warum brauche ich nur
so lange, Dir zu sagen,
dass ich Schwierigkeiten
mit der Kommunikation
habe?

© ASHLEIGH BRILLIANT 1983 SANTA BARBARA.

POT-SHOTS NO 2918

IT'S HOPELESS!

TOMORROW
THERE'LL BE
EVEN MORE BOOKS
I SHOULD HAVE READ
THAN
THERE ARE
TODAY.

Es ist zum Verzweifeln!
Morgen gibt es noch mehr
Bücher, als heute,
die ich hätte lesen sollen.

Im Krieg zwischen Gut und Böse desertierte ich, aber ich kann mich nicht mehr erinnern, auf welcher Seite ich gekämpft habe.

Und was tun Sie, um den globalen Mangel an Lebensfreude zu beheben?

Wie gut meine Darstellung ist, hängt manchmal davon ab wie gut mein Publikum ist.

Wenn Ihnen die Menschen
alle sehr freundlich
vorkommen, gehen sie
wahrscheinlich mit den
falschen Leuten um.

Als Geste des guten Willens
will ich davon Abstand
nehmen, Ihnen die Zähne
einzuschlagen.

Muss ich meinen gesunden
Menschenverstand aufs Spiel
setzen, um Dir Deinen
zu retten?

146

© ASHLEIGH BRILLIANT 1990. Ashleigh Brilliant SANTA BARBARA   POT-SHOTS NO 5302.

**I KNOW I'M BEING FAIR**

**when both sides accuse me of unfairness.**

Wenn beide Seiten mich der Ungerechtigkeit bezichtigen, weiss ich, dass ich Gerechtigkeit übe.

© ASHLEIGH BRILLIANT 1991.   POT-SHOTS NO. 5538.

**THIS COULD HAVE BEEN A PERFECT WORLD ~**

**BUT THEN YOU AND I WOULD NEVER HAVE BEEN ADMITTED.**

Ashleigh Brilliant
SANTA BARBARA

Es hätte die vollkommene Welt werden können, aber dann hätte man Dir und mir den Eintritt verwehrt.

© ASHLEIGH BRILLIANT 1991.   POT-SHOTS NO. 5440.

**I HEREBY LEAVE MY PARKING-PLACE**

**TO THE FASTEST, THE BRAVEST, AND THE STRONGEST.**

Ashleigh Brilliant
SANTA BARBARA

Ich hinterlasse hiermit meine Parklücke, zugunsten des Schnellsten, Mutigsten und Stärksten.

POT-SHOTS NO. 5455. ©ASHLEIGH BRILLIANT 1991.

**REASON SHOULD NOT BE RESORTED TO UNTIL ALL ATTEMPTS AT A SOLUTION BY FORCE HAVE BEEN EXHAUSTED.**

*Ashleigh Brilliant*
SANTA BARBARA

Man soll sich erst der Vernunft bedienen, bis alle versuchung eine gewaltige Lösung zu erreichen ausprobiert waren.

©ASHLEIGH BRILLIANT 1991.   POT-SHOTS NO. 5546.

**IT COMFORTS ME TO KNOW OTHERS ARE SUFFERING TOO.**

**BUT IT DOESN'T MAKE THE PAIN GO AWAY.**

*Ashleigh Brilliant*
SANTA BARBARA

Es ist mir ein Trost, dass andere auch leiden, aber das stillt den Schmerz noch lange nicht.

©ASHLEIGH BRILLIANT 1991.   POT-SHOTS NO 5587.

**THE ONLY GOOD THING ABOUT ANGER**

**IS THAT IT PROVES YOU HAVE FEELINGS.**

*Ashleigh Brilliant*
SANTA BARBARA

Das einzig Gute an einem Wutausbruch ist, es zeigt, dass man Gefühle hat.

© ASHLEIGH BRILLIANT 1991.    POT-SHOTS NO. 5618.

# IF YOU ALWAYS TELL THE TRUTH,

nobody will trust you.

Ashleigh Brilliant
SANTA BARBARA

Wer stets
die Wahrheit sagt,
dem traut man nicht.

© ASHLEIGH BRILLIANT 1992.    POT-SHOTS NO. 5920.

# HOW CAN I HAVE SO LITTLE PRIVACY,

## AND YET FEEL SO ALONE?

Ashleigh Brilliant
SANTA BARBARA

Wie kommt es,
dass ich fast kein Privatleben
habe, und trotzdem
so einsam bin?

© ASHLEIGH BRILLIANT 1992.    POT-SHOTS NO. 5708.

# I LIKE HAVING SOMEWHERE TO GO,

BECAUSE
IT ALSO
GIVES ME
SOMEWHERE
TO
COME BACK
FROM.

Ashleigh Brilliant
SANTA BARBARA

Es ist gut
ein Ziel zu haben,
dann weiss ich
von Wo ich zurückkehre.

© ASHLEIGH BRILLIANT 1992. *Ashleigh Brilliant* SANTA BARBARA    POT-SHOTS NO. 5788.

## STATUES OF POPULAR HEROES

### SHOULD ALWAYS BE EASILY REMOVEABLE AND REPLACEABLE.

Denkmäler von Volkshelden
sollten stets leicht
zu entfernen
und zu ersetzen sein.

POT-SHOTS NO. 5837.    © ASHLEIGH BRILLIANT 1992.

## GOOD TEACHERS AND GOOD STUDENTS

### DON'T GET EACH OTHER AS OFTEN AS THEY DESERVE TO.

*Ashleigh Brilliant*
SANTA BARBARA

Gute Lehrer
und gute Schüler
finden sich
nicht so oft wie sie sollten.

© ASHLEIGH BRILLIANT 1992    POT-SHOTS NO. 5697.

## IT'S BETTER TO RISK TRUSTING THE WRONG PEOPLE

### THAN NEVER TO TRUST ANYBODY AT ALL.

Es ist besser, dass man es
riskiert, den falschen
Leuten zu trauen,
als überhaupt
nie jemandem zu trauen.

© ASHLEIGH BRILLIANT 1992.

POT-SHOTS NO. 5906.

**I RESERVE THE RIGHT**

TO REFUSE TO PLAY ANYBODY WHO KNOWS HOW TO PREVENT ME FROM CHEATING.

Ashleigh Brilliant
SANTA BARBARA

Ich behalte mir das Recht vor, mit niemandem zu spielen, der weiss, wie man mich vom Schummeln abhält.

© ASHLEIGH BRILLIANT 1992.

POT-SHOTS NO. 5833.

*Almost everywhere, there is fertile soil for planting praise and encouragement.*

Ashleigh Brilliant
SANTA BARBARA

Fruchtbaren Boden für den Anbau von Lob und Ermutigung gibt es überall.

© ASHLEIGH BRILLIANT 1990.
SANTA BARBARA

POT-SHOTS NO. 5133.

**DON'T WORRY ABOUT LEAVING YOUR TROUBLES BEHIND ~**

THEY'LL ALL STILL BE THERE WHEN YOU GET BACK.

Ashleigh Brilliant

Lassen Sie ruhig Ihre Schwierigkeiten hinter sich—bei Ihrer Rückkehr werden sie auf Sie warten.

# Pot-Shots BY ASHLEIGH BRILLIANT

© ASHLEIGH BRILLIANT 1981. SANTA BARBARA.

POT-SHOTS NO. 2210.

I make occasional visits to Reality,

but I'm not

a full-time resident.

Ashleigh Brilliant

Ich mache gelegentlich
Abstecher in die Wirklichkeit,
sie ist jedoch nicht
mein ständiger Wohnort

# XII. It All Deep Ends

Here we are, approaching the end of the book, and it turns out to be the deep end, containing a curious assortment of (I hope not unpalatably) profound thoughts. But one of the peculiarities of thought is that it can be both deep and elevated at the same time. Ours is a universe in which the terrain is still so mysterious that nobody can clearly distinguish the depths from the heights. What does seem clear, however, is that the same space which appears to separate any two points in it (or, for that matter, any two persons), can also be seen as a potential pathway between them.

With that stupendous insight (itself worth the entire price of the book), our brief exploration of Communication must now wind up (or down). From here on, please allow your head to swim in any direction it chooses. But, whatever your compass heading, I hope it may turn out to be along some great circle which will ultimately bring you back within my orbit.

If you insist that I leave you on terra firma, be assured that, at least as far as this planet is concerned, no matter where you and I may stand, we stand on common ground. And if, in any meaningful way, our minds have meshed on these pages, it can only be because, regardless of all evidence to the contrary, in some very basic sense we really do all speak the same language.

© ASHLEIGH BRILLIANT 1992  POT-SHOTS NO. 5642.

## IT MAY BE
## LATER THAN WE THINK,

OR IT MAY BE
EARLIER
THAN WE CAN POSSIBLY IMAGINE.

Entweder es ist
später als du denkst,
oder es ist früher
als du dir vorstellen kannst.

---

© ASHLEIGH BRILLIANT 1979  POT-SHOTS NO. 1615.

There's only one thing
more beautiful than
a beautiful dream,

and that's
a beautiful reality.

Es gibt nur eins,
was schöner ist
als ein schöner Traum:
eine schöne Wirklichkeit.

---

© ASHLEIGH BRILLIANT 1980  SANTA BARBARA  POT-SHOTS NO. 1845

HOW CAN
WE BE
MADE OF
THINGS
SO SMALL,

YET
STILL BE
PART OF
THINGS
SO LARGE?

Wie kommt es, dass wir
aus so winzigen Elementen
bestehen, und wir doch
Teile eines so riesigen
Ganzen sind?

POT-SHOTS NO 1863

IT
TROUBLES ME
THAT
I HAVE
NO WAY
OF KNOWING
WHAT
I HAVE
NO
WAY
OF KNOWING.

©ASHLEIGH BRILLIANT 1980. SANTA BARBARA.

Es stört mich,
dass ich nicht wissen kann,
was ich nicht wissen kann.

©ASHLEIGH BRILLIANT 1980 SANTA BARBARA.

POT-SHOTS NO 1974

DON'T CROSS OVER

UNTIL
YOU'RE
SURE

THERE'S
ANOTHER
SIDE.

Überquere nicht
bis Du sicher bist
ein Drüben existiert.

©ASHLEIGH BRILLIANT 1982.
SANTA BARBARA.

POT-SHOTS NO. 2454.

I BELONG

TO
THE
UNIVERSE,

BUT
AM NOT SURE
EXACTLY
WHAT
PRIVILEGES
THAT
ENTITLES ME TO.

Ich bin Mitglied des
Universums, aber über
dessen Privilegien bin ich im
Ungewissen.

THE
EARTH
MAKES A
PLEASANT
RESTING—
SPOT,

When
you're
on your way
somewhere else.

© ASHLEIGH BRILLIANT 1983
SANTA BARBARA

POT- SHOTS NO. 2990.

Die Erde is ein angenehmer Ruheplatz, wenn man woanders hin unterwegs ist.

© ASHLEIGH BRILLIANT 1991.

POT- SHOTS NO. 5517.

CONGRATULATE
ME!

I've just had
another
narrow
escape
from reality.

Sie dürfen mir gratulieren! Ich bin der Wirklichkeit wiedermal knapp entronnen.

© ASHLEIGH BRILLIANT 1983.  SANTA BARBARA.

POT- SHOTS NO. 2953.

MY LIFETIME
IS JUST A MOMENT
IN ETERNITY ~

BUT FOR ME
IT'S QUITE
AN IMPORTANT
MOMENT.

Auch wenn mein Leben nur ein Augenblick in der Ewigkeit ist, für mich ist es ein ziemlich wichtiger Augenblick.

© ASHLEIGH BRILLIANT 1985.
SANTA BARBARA

POT-SHOTS NO. 3524.

ON THE QUESTION OF WHETHER OR NOT I REALLY EXIST,

I'M TAKING A WAIT-AND-SEE ATTITUDE.

Ashleigh Brilliant

In der Frage,
existiere ich nun wirklich
oder nicht,
heisst es für mich: abwarten.

© ASHLEIGH BRILLIANT 1990.
SANTA BARBARA

POT-SHOTS NO. 5030.

BIG THINGS DON'T SCARE ME:

THE ATOMS IN MY BODY OUTNUMBER THE STARS IN THE UNIVERSE.

Ashleigh Brilliant

Grösse schreckt mich nicht:
mein Körper besteht
aus mehr Atomen
als es Sterne im Universum
gibt.

POT-SHOTS NO. 5052.

I WISH WE COULD BRING BACK THE GOOD OLD DAYS,

WHEN THE SUN WENT

AROUND THE EARTH.

Ashleigh Brilliant
SANTA BARBARA

© ASHLEIGH BRILLIANT 1990.

Manchmal wünsche ich mir,
die alten Tage kämen wieder,
als die Sonne sich noch
um die Erde drehte.

POT-SHOTS NO. 5058. ©ASHLEIGH BRILLIANT 1990. *Ashleigh Brilliant* SANTA BARBARA

## HOW CAN I BE SURE WHICH WILL BE MY LAST DAY ON EARTH, until the following day?

Wie kann ich sicher sein
es ist mein letzter Tag
auf dieser Erde, bevor der
folgende Tag heran ist?

©ASHLEIGH BRILLIANT 1990. POT-SHOTS NO. 5154.

## The only truly solid foundation there can be for anything in this world is solid faith.

*Ashleigh Brilliant* SANTA BARBARA

Die einzige wirklich solide
Basis, die es in dieser
Welt gibt, is ein
unerschütterlicher Glaube.

©ASHLEIGH BRILLIANT 1990. POT-SHOTS NO. 5305.

## ALWAYS ASK GOD FOR MORE THAN YOU REALLY WANT ~ THAT WILL LEAVE SOME ROOM FOR NEGOTIATING.

*Ashleigh Brilliant* SANTA BARBARA

Man soll den lieben Gott
immer um mehr bitten
als man eigentlich will;
auf die Weise schafft man
sich Verhandlungsspielraum

© ASHLEIGH BRILLIANT 1990.

POT-SHOTS NO. 5111.

Just because we're not immortal doesn't mean we're not eternal.

Wir mögen nicht unsterblich sein, aber das heisst noch lange nicht, das wir nicht ewig sind.

© ASHLEIGH BRILLIANT 1991.

POT-SHOTS NO. 5388.

DID GOD WANT US TO DISCOVER OUR OWN PURPOSE, OR DID HE SIMPLY FORGET TO TELL US?

Wollte der liebe Gott, dass wir den Sinn des Lebens selbst suchen, oder hat er nur vergessen, ihn uns mitzuteilen?

© ASHLEIGH BRILLIANT 1991.

POT-SHOTS NO. 5425.

GOD HAS RESIGNED FROM THE UNIVERSE, AND ASKED THAT HIS NAME NOT BE INCLUDED IN THE CREDITS.

Gott hat sich aus dem Universum zurückgezogen, und darum gebeten dass sein Name bei den Schlusstiteln unerwähnt bleibt.

Neuesten astronomischen
Erkenntnissen zufolge
befindet sich das Universum
in einem Zustand
der Veränderung.

Warum sieht man immer
so viel klarer,
wenn man sich nicht
inmitten der Dinge befindet?

Ich bezweifle,
dass es klug wäre,
sich dem Universum
gnadeflehend zu Füssen
zu werfen.

Das Leben ist wohl
kaum ein Rätsel,
das alle Hinweise zu seiner
Lösung mitliefert.

Warum ist Hoffnung
so viel einfacher
als Glaube?

Die Unvermeidlichkeit
des Todes
ist wohl der grösste
Aberglaube der uns
verbleibt.

© ASHLEIGH BRILLIANT 1992    POT SHOTS NO 5786

WHY ARE THE MOST DIFFICULT QUESTIONS ALWAYS THE ONES THAT BEGIN WITH WHY?

Warum sind die schwierigsten Fragen stets diejenigen, die mit "warum" beginnen?

© ASHLEIGH BRILLIANT 1992    POT-SHOTS NO. 5937.

MIRACLES DO HAPPEN, BUT NOT OFTEN ENOUGH TO BE WORTH WAITING UP FOR.

Wunder geschehen, aber nicht oft genug, dass es sich lohnt Schlaf zu verlieren, um auf sie zu warten.

© ASHLEIGH BRILLIANT 1992    POT-SHOTS NO. 5960.

CAN GOD MAKE MISTAKES? IF SO, IT WOULD EXPLAIN MANY OTHERWISE VERY PUZZLING THINGS.

Macht Gott Fehler? ja, wäre das die Erklärung für viele Rätsel des Lebens.

POT-SHOTS NO 6014

# I DON'T LIKE PLAYING GAMES WITH GOD ~

### HE'S SUCH A POOR LOSER.

*Ashleigh Brilliant*

Mit Gott zu spielen
ist kein Spass—
er ist ein schlechter
Verlierer.

# OF COURSE THERE'S A HEAVEN ~

### BUT I DON'T THINK YOU CAN GET THERE FROM HERE.

*Ashleigh Brilliant*
SANTA BARBARA

Selbsverständlich gibt
es einen Himmel—
nur führt von hier
vielleicht kein Weg dorthin.

POT-SHOTS NO 5677.

# IF YOU ALWAYS WANTED TO LIVE IN A VERY BIG UNIVERSE, SCIENCE HAS WONDERFUL NEWS FOR YOU.

*Ashleigh Brilliant*
SANTA BARBARA

Wenn Sie schon immer in
einem unvorstellbar grossen
Universum leben wollten,
dann hat die
Wissenschaft gute
Nachrichten für Sie.

# Permission Fruition

Pot-Shots® *per se* have (lamentably) not yet, to my knowledge, become required reading in any educational institution. But, of the numerous requests I receive for permission to quote or reproduce one or more of them, many come from writers of textbooks and other scholars, or from publications which are in other ways connected with the advancement of learning and the shaping of young and impressionable minds. The following list of such materials, in all of which Brilliant Thoughts® are used by special permission (often very creatively and as cleverly apropos illustrations), will give you some idea of the many forms in which these proposals have borne fruit.

Adler, Ronald B., and Neil Towne. *Looking Out/Looking In: Interpersonal Communication.* New York: Holt, Rinehart and Winston, 1987. [College-level textbook.]

Anchor Bay School District, Special Services. *Connection.* New Baltimore, Michigan, 1991. [Newsletter.]

Ardell, Donald B., and John G. Langdon. *Wellness: The Body, Mind, and Spirit.* Dubuque: Kendall/Hunt, 1989. [University of Central Florida, Orlando, Health and Sports manual.]

Arkoff, Abe. *The Illuminated Life.* New York: Allyn & Bacon, 1994. [College-level Psychology textbook in Adjustment and Personal Growth.]

Black, Jan Knippers. *Development in Theory and Practice: Bridging the Gap.* Westview Press, 1991.

Boswell, John C. *Garule Wali.* Walgett High School, Walgett, New South Wales, Australia, 1992. [Curriculum Document.]

Brown, Mark, and Julius Laffal. *Coping With Mental Disturbance.* Middletown, Connecticut: Dept. of Psychology, Connecticut Valley Hospital, 1983. [Workbook.]

Canberra College of Advanced Education, Health Education Dept. *Salutogenic Newsletter.* Belconnen, A.C.T., Australia, 1986-87.

*East Detroiter.* East Detroit High School, East Detroit, Michigan, 1977. [Yearbook.]

*El Potrillo.* Silver High School, Silver City, New Mexico, 1992. [Yearbook.].

European Society for Photobiology. *Newsletter.* Royal Military College, Kingston, Ontario, Canada, Department of Chemistry, 1992-

Faribault Technical Institute. *1988-89 Student Handbook.* Faribault, Minnesota, 1988.

Gardner, Kenneth D. Jr., M.D. "Pardon Me, But Can You Show Me a Nephrologist?" in *American Journal of Kidney Diseases,* Vol. 1, No. 5, March 1982, p. 259.

Geigold, William C. *Management by Objectives.* New York: McGraw-Hill, 1978. [Management textbook.]

Giles, Howard, and Nikolas Coupland. "Language Attitudes: Discursive, Contextual, and Gerontological Considerations," in Reynolds, A.G. (ed.) *McGill Conference on Bilingualism, Multiculturalism, and Second Language Learning: A Tribute to Wallace E. Lambert.* Hillsdale, New Jersey: Erlbaum, 1990. [Chapter in a festschrift.]

Goleman, Daniel, Trygg Engen, and Anthony Davids. *Introductory Psychology.* New York: Random House, 1982. [College-level textbook.]

Greenfield School, Student Environmental Alliance. *SEA Newsletter.* Greenfield, California, 1990.

Habel, Lowell *et. al.* "Speech 102: Theory and Method of Communication." University of California, Santa Barbara, 1981. [Course outline.]

Heinich, Robert, Michael Molenda, and James D. Russell. *Instructional Media.* New York: John Wiley & Sons, 1982. [Education Text book].

Hofstadter, Douglas R. *Mathemagical Themas: Questing for the Essence of Mind and Pattern.* New York: Basic Books, 1985. [Essays.]

Houdart, Francoise. *People, Book 1* (1974), *People, Book 2* (1976), and *Meeting People* (1982). Paris, France: Hatier. [French text-book series for teaching English.]

John Wiley & Sons Canada Ltd. *Entrepreneurship: Creating a Venture.* Rexdale, Ontario, 1990. [High school textbook.]

Leong, Lim Chong. "My Child Is Smart." *Grow.* Republic of Singapore: Ministry of Education, April, 1980. [Magazine for parents and teachers.]

Lial, Margaret L., and Charles D. Miller. *Calculus With Applications.* Glenview, Ilinois: Scott, Foresman, 1989. [College-level Mathematics textbook.]

Lutheran Campus Ministry. *Newsletter.* Southwest Texas State University, San Marcos, Texas, 1976-83.

Macksville High School. *Bulletin.* Macksville, New South Wales, Australia, 1989.

Massey University, Department of Accountancy. *Newsletter.* Palmerston North, New Zealand, 1992-

Meyer, Dennis R. "Introduction to Transforming Congregational Conflict Through the Six Steps to Nonviolent Social Change." State University of New York, Albany NY, 1992. [Doctoral Thesis.]

Mosak, Harold H. *Ha Ha and Aha: The Role of Humor in Psychotherapy.* Muncie, Indiana: Accelerated Development Inc., 1987. [Monograph.]

National College of Chiropractic. *The Synapse.* Chicago, 1980-81. [Student newspaper.]

New South Wales Government Dept. of Education, Board of Senior School Studies. *Modern History.* Sydney, Australia, 1986. [Specimen examination papers and guidelines.]

Oregon State University, College of Home Economics. *Oregon Parenthood Education Curriculum Guide.* Corvallis, Oregon, 1990.

Purdue Lutheran Ministry. *The Link.* West Lafayette, Indiana, 1984. [Newsletter.]

Regent College. *Summer Daily.* Vancouver, British Columbia, Canada, 1991. [News bulletin.]

Rigby Heinemann. *Into Fiction, Book 2.* Port Melbourne, Australia: 1993. [Secondary school textbook.]

Rossi, Suzanne S., and Shirley S. Schiff. "A Handbook For Parents of Special Children." California Lutheran College, Thousand Oaks California, 1984. [M.Sc. Thesis in Education.]

Rutgers University, Philosophy Club. *Rutgers Philosophical Reader.* New Brunswick, New Jersey, 1983-84.

Schaie, K. Warner, and James Geiwitz. *Adult Development and Aging.* Boston: Little, Brown, 1982. [College-level textbook.]

Swan, Michael. *Kaleidoscope.* Cambridge, England: Cambridge University Press, 1979. [An anthology of English for non-native speakers.]

Tripp, Robert L. The Game of School. Reston, Virginia: Extended Vision Press, 1993. [Monograph.]

University of Alaska Southeast. *Double Eagle.* Ketchikan, Alaska, 1990. [Newsletter.]

University of British Columbia, Faculty of Education. *S.I. Network Newsletter.* Vancouver, Canada, 1991. [Newsletter for Science teachers.]
Univerrsity of California, Berkeley, Career Planning and Placement Center. *Career Planning Guide, 1992-1993.*

The above list, set before you with I hope pardonable pride, includes only printed materials, and so does not mention the many additional educational uses of Brilliant Thoughts as projected images or oral quotations in lectures. And Education is only one area in which this material is being found useful. Other particularly fertile fields include Health, Religion, and Business. If you have ideas of your own for making use of any of my copyrighted material, the Ashleigh Brilliant Permissions Department will be very happy to hear from you. (See address, p. 167.)

# Over to You

Did we really communicate here? Do you feel like saying "Don't stop!"? O.K., I won't—not if you keep sending me encouraging signals. How can you best do that?—by getting in on my act from your end. This book is just part of a very special Ashleigh Brilliant Communication System, which you yourself can quite easily and enjoyably incorporate into your life.

There are now thousands of Brilliant Thoughts®, to help you express your own thoughts and feelings in every imaginable situation and relationship, and on all kinds of occasions. They are all available on individual postcards, and you can indefinitely prolong the pleasure of our encounter here by giving yourself the fun of choosing the very best and most appropriate messages for all your own communication needs.

You are hereby politely urged to send for my catalogue, which comes with sample cards and an inviting order-form, and also includes information about my many other books and products. The current (1994) price is two U.S. dollars. Please enclose that amount, or its equivalent in your own time and currency.

My address is:

Ashleigh Brilliant
117 W. Valerio Street
Santa Barbara, California 93101, U.S.A.